EVA PERÓN

THE MYTHS OF A WOMAN

EVA PERÓN

THE MYTHS OF A WOMAN

J. M. TAYLOR

THE UNIVERSITY OF CHICAGO PRESS

The University of Chicago Press, Chicago 60637

Basil Blackwell, Oxford

Published 1979

83 82 81 80 79 5 4 3 2 1

Library of Congress Cataloging in Publication Data

Taylor, Julie M
  Eva Perón, the myths of a woman.

  Bibliography:
    1. Perón, Eva Duarte, 1919-1952. 2. Argentine
Republic—Presidents—Wives—Biography. 3. Politicians—
Argentine Republic—Biography. 4. Argentine Republic—
Politics and goverment—1943-1955. 5. Peronism.
I. Title.
F2849.P37T39   982'.06'0924 [B]   79.19547
ISBN 0-226-79143-2

Printed in the United States of America

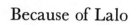
Because of Lalo

Contents

Acknowledgments

To the many Argentinians who inspired and formed this work go my profound thanks. The political turmoil that continues in Argentina renders impossible their individual recognition. Nevertheless, the concern and companionship of those who helped me as colleagues and informants, often assuming both roles simultaneously, cannot go unnoticed.

This final product represents, as well, the contributions of many institutions: St. Antony's College, Oxford University, which in the beginning made it possible for me to initiate research into the case of Eva Perón and in the end supported the writing of the completed study; the Ford Foundation Foreign Area Program, which funded fieldwork in Buenos Aires for eighteen months; Oxford University, which provided a grant-in-aid for the final months of the production of the work as a dissertation; and the University of California, San Diego, which offered me the time to write the study as a book.

To the historians who have taken an active interest in this essentially anthropological work, I owe a special debt. Ezequiel Gallo aided immeasurably at Oxford in the original conception of the work. He continued throughout the years to help in the formulation of the historical aspects of the study and to relate them to an anthropological approach. Tulio Halperín Donghi offered crucial stimulus and supervision of the initial steps of the study until it was well under way in the field. The painstaking care of Donald Peck in his reading of the manuscript and in his resulting comments invariably proved fruitful.

The book has taken its final form thanks to the encouragement and meticulous criticism of F. G. Bailey, who provided invaluable lessons in the craft of writing a book.

Throughout the course of this study, Rodney Needham and Peter Rivière have made their presence so deeply felt as mentors and as friends that I can conceive of neither my work nor my world without them. For their continuing inspiration and support they have my deepest gratitude.

Several conditions had met in the Lady of Quetcham which to the reasoners in that neighbourhood seemed to have an essential connection with each other. It was occasionally recalled that she had been the heiress of a fortune gained by some moist or dry business in the city, in order fully to account for her having a squat figure, a harsh parrot-like voice, and a systematically high head-dress; and since these points made her externally rather ridiculous, it appeared to many only natural that she should have what are called literary tendencies. A little comparison would have shown that all these points are to be found apart; daughters of aldermen being often well-grown and well-featured, pretty women having sometimes harsh or husky voices, and the production of feeble literature being found compatible with the most diverse forms of *physique*, masculine as well as feminine.

GEORGE ELIOT, *Daniel Deronda*

In the enlightened world, mythology has entered into the profane. In its blank purity, the reality which has been cleansed of demons and their conceptual descendants assumes the numinous character which the ancient world attributed to demons. Under the title of brute facts, the social injustice from which they proceed is now as assuredly sacred a preserve as the medicine man was sacrosanct by reason of the protection of his goals.

MAX HORKHEIMER and THEODORE W. ADORNO
Dialectic of Enlightenment
('The Concept of Enlightenment')

Introduction
The Myth of the Myth

Since the Argentinians speak of 'the myth of Eva Perón', and anthropologists have long considered themselves to have something special to offer in the study of myth, it seemed logical (to both Argentinians and anthropologists) that I should observe the myth of this popular leader. Evita Perón, who rose from humble origins to international renown as First Lady of Argentina at the side of her husband Juan Perón, inspired such loyalty among her people that two decades after her death she remained the heroine of the working classes and political dynamite in Argentina. Armed with anthropology's literature on myth and its methods of field work, I arrived in Argentina in late 1970, settled in with a working class Peronist family, and waited to participate in its community life and to identify and observe the myth of Eva and its part in this life.

Both in Argentina and abroad, it was widely believed that the myth of Evita had arisen in the Argentinian working classes and centred an ideal of pure and passive womanhood incarnate, who exercised saintly power closely related to this classic femininity. According to this idea, popular enthusiasm for Eva Perón not only assumes a vaguely religious nature, but also takes the form of an irrational, mystic reverence for a saint or madonna. Peronists and anti-Peronists, Argentinians and foreigners alike, have assumed that the masses of popular Peronism hail the figure of Eva much like that of the heroine of party propaganda, the Lady of Hope. It was this view, represented by virtually all sources, that defined the phenomenon I set out to study. But such a view presented unexpected problems. [1]

Its parallels with the official Lady of Hope made it obvious that the myth of Eva had also been important in political propaganda, where it had been manipulated by specialists dedicated solely to the task. The culture of professional propagandists and journalists is not usually that of the sector to which other groups in Argentina attribute the creation of the mystic myth of Eva Perón: the lowest socio-economic strata of society. Yet it is always possible that popular versions may be based on propaganda or may incorporate elements from it. My task at the outset, was to define the working class myth of Eva Perón and to discover its connections with Peronist propaganda.

This relationship confronted me with another problem particular to anthropological studies in complex societies. Argentina is a highly literate society. No investigator can ignore the fact that the Argentinians read: they read political propaganda, commercial publicity, popular and serious literature and history. Yet for answers to all the questions this fact poses, the anthropologist cannot rely solely on a content analysis of different media. The observer must also scrutinize carefully the resonances of themes among various categories of people. Documents of whatever sort cannot be examined in isolation from a field situation. One must look not only for themes, but also for the ideas and values that the members of the culture associate with them. Thus echoes in the popular oral versions of a myth become the criteria for selecting written sources to study.

The problem of the connection between a myth, those who believe in it, and the professional image makers shaped and subsequently modified my plan of research. I had intended to live in a working class Peronist community while I examined the current media and that of the first Peronist regime. I would then be able to compare versions of the myth emerging from official propaganda both with popular literature and with versions collected from interviews with working class Peronist informants. But these plans had to be modified when I discovered that parallel investigations were yielding, instead of parallel accounts, versions which differed from each other in very significant ways.

In order to examine themes in the myth of Eva Perón both in the Argentinian media and in the social sector to which I supposed them most relevant, I used two major sources. First, I systematically reviewed newspapers, periodicals and popular literature, both from the period contemporary to my stay and from the time between the rise of the Peróns in 1945 to Eva's death in 1952. In a literate society, these sources do not replace oral traditions, but become their indispensable complement. Daily papers and popular literature form an important part of life in Buenos Aires. My investigations included a complete reading of *Democracia*, the major organ of the press of the Peronist regime, and of the accessible collections of other papers of the regime and its opposition. Of the popular literature examined, the Peronist sources covered the first Peronist regime and the period after the proscription on Peronism was lifted in the early 1970s. Amongst the earlier sources a large collection of Peronist school texts was important.

My second source was the working class family with whom I lived, their neighbours and their friends. During Perón's first period in power they had occupied a place in the lower socio-economic strata of Buenos Aires. Although the family was increasingly upwardly mobile, with children and grandchildren moving into the middle class, the members still exhibited many traits of the working classes. They lived in a large and ancient apartment building, which had become a tenement. The owners of the apartments in this building had for the most part lived there since Perón's time. Many tenants, like my family, had settled there upon arriving from an interior province. With many experiences and years of co-existence in common, these families formed something like a community united by more than the formal bond that brought them together for regular meetings as co-owners of the building.

All the apartments in this building were similar: with two bedrooms, a tiny kitchen, and an equally minuscule bathroom all opening onto a corridor. This connecting passageway was protected from the damp cold and rain of the riverside city's winter by a canvas awning that flapped violently in the windy winter storms. When I moved in, only my family, of all those in the building, had replaced this canvas with sliding glass windows. These they nevertheless often kept open in order to keep up on the affairs of their neighbours, who were always audible through the air shaft shared by the inside apartments. There was no hot water, nor any shower or bath. We would give ourselves what the mother of the family called a 'horse bath' by tossing buckets of water—which, if time permitted, we heated on the stove—over ourselves, pushing the water that then flooded the bathroom down a floor drain with a long handled squeegee device. Winter made this process an ordeal, for there was no heat other than a small kerosene stove. In such an apartment, the father and mother of my family had raised their six children.

After several months in the building, I began to suspect what more than a year of further residence would confirm: few, if any, tales of a mystical and saintly Eva Perón were to be heard from this group or among the other similar working class groups I met through my neighbours. This called for a much more complex definition of the myth of Eva Perón. In fact belief in the mystic content and the working class locus of the myth of Eva Perón were parts of the myth itself: another social sector had generated this version about the working classes and their mystical attraction to Eva Perón.

Thus, while the media which I was examining at the time waxed eloquent on the mystic and fanatical beliefs about Eva Perón found among the working classes, I found little evidence of such beliefs amongst my working class informants. However, they had different versions of her significance. Most had had some contact with Evita. They discussed her in realistic terms. Almost everyone had received or known someone who had received some personal aid from her—a sewing machine, a bed, some medicine, money on which to marry. She had advocated such-and-such a law, they would state, and they would then launch into a discussion of the change in conditions that this had brought about. The foundation she established had provided necessities and had even fought inflation. Eva had instigated the building of housing for the poor, in which relatives or friends of my informants still lived. The list continued, but it never portrayed the accomplishments of Evita Perón in association with an ideally chaste and submissive femininity or emanating from the mystic powers of a woman, a saint, and a martyr.

Further, my working class informants summarily dismissed versions of the myth which, according to newspapers, pamphlets, texts, and books, they were supposed to have generated. The talk would turn quickly away from the saint and madonna and return to the concrete benefits Eva had provided. On only one element was there agreement: to do what she had done, Eva had made great personal sacrifices. Yet while they admired this sacrifice, it did not take on the religious aura of martyrdom.

At other times the working people offered an image of Eva that seemed to contradict more definitively still the idea of a classically feminine saint. Amongst factory workers in other parts of the city, I met for the first time the aggressive warrior and battle companion of the urban guerrilla, the revolutionary Eva Perón. This Eva inspired the loyalty of factions from socially diverse backgrounds who were the new Peronists of the late 1960s and early 1970s. Workers who went beyond a realistic assessment of Eva's importance in their lives turned to the Revolutionary before they turned to the Lady of Hope.

Long term residence, participant observation in one small-scale community to examine questions pertinent to a larger society, and open-ended interviews in depth—the usual anthropological techniques—provided knowledge that had proved otherwise inaccessible. Yet the Argentinian political situation made interviewing amongst the working classes difficult. I arrived before the proscription on Peronism, maintained by anti-Peronist governments after the fall of Perón, had been lifted, and people beyond my immediate community and its contacts were afraid to discuss Eva Perón with anyone. A North American who brought up the subject disturbed them still more. Yet within the community in which I lived, my close contact with its life and members gradually established that rapport through which a fieldworker seeks his information. No one interested in the myth of Eva Perón had as yet been close enough to the working classes to notice that their version of Eva Perón could vary strikingly from versions generally known elsewhere as 'the myth of Eva Perón'. But can one be sure that the community studied was indeed typical of a larger sector? To test the wider interpretative value of my studies, I focused the remainder of my study on the middle classes.

I had been confused at first by contact with Peronist informants who purported to be working class, and who did in fact produce the mystical version of Eva's life and significance which coincided with accounts in the media from both anti-Peronist and Peronist sources. However, I gradually realized that I was hearing their version much less frequently than others. Upon re-examination, their similar images proved to have come from a different social sector altogether, represented by labour leaders, politicians, propagandists, and the small group of wealthy industrialists and landowners who were members of the Peronist party. This myth did not parallel official propaganda by chance: the propaganda itself had emerged from the social sector whose members earnestly recounted to me variations on the same themes. Argentinian standards define this sector as middle class. Thus the locus of the images of 'Santa Evita' was established as the middle classes.

Meanwhile, the themes collected from the media presented striking similarities with versions of the myth of Eva Perón from yet another source, one which was providing me with a growing collection of images: the anti-Peronist middle and upper classes of Buenos Aires. Argentinians themselves often referred collectively to the negative imagery of these groups as the Black Myth of Eva Perón. I had discovered quickly that I was not the only one seeking to explain a myth of Eva current among what was known as the 'Peronist masses'. Argentinians who considered themselves higher in social status also assumed that much of the lasting loyalty of the working classes to Juan and Evita Perón was due to quasi-religious myths concerning Eva's mystical powers. When anti-Peronist Argentinians of the upper and middle classes discovered my interest in the subject, they reported their findings to me. As they recounted details remembered over the quarter century since the beginnings of the first Peronist regime, I saw they had clearly been interested in the myth of Eva Perón for a long time. They insisted that the myth of a mystical Eva had never died among the working classes, and no new anecdote on the subject escaped them. Yet the increasingly obvious presence in the working class community in which I lived of a realistic and sometimes revolutionary Eva in the place of a madonna figure provided a marked contrast with their stories.

Gradually, then, as the wealth of detail on the madonna filled my notebooks, the weight given the different aspects of my investigations shifted. It had become clear that realistic versions of the power and accomplishments of Eva Perón found in the working classes differed from the mystic versions attributed to them by others. Accounts of semi-religious power exercised by Eva over her popular following were pouring in from the middle and upper classes. This led me to a closer investigation of the images of 'Santa Evita' and her magnetism among the masses. For the last half-year of my fieldwork I decided to live with an upper-middle class family in Buenos Aires, who, with their extended network of relatives and friends, added significantly to the anti-Peronist versions of the pseudo-saint and her gullible following which I had already gathered. I extended my reading to include the anti-Peronist literature that began to appear after the fall of Perón and continues today. During this period I also interviewed people from the middle-class Peronist sector mentioned earlier, which had provided me with Peronist versions of a similar, although differently valued, relation between saintly martyr and innocently devout populace.

These accounts from groups of distinct political persuasions had to this point been generally believed to represent different myths. But I would argue that, in ways to be examined in the body of this work, they express precisely the same values. The focus of Peronist and anti-Peronist versions on the same themes demonstrated that Peronist propaganda and Peronist and anti-Peronist myths of the mystical Eva were directly related, not to any phenomenon in the Peronist working classes, but to important middle class Argentinian values. The problem was no longer one of how propaganda had manipulated working class values and imagery. I needed now to explore the ways in which middle class propagandists had helped to construct an image reflecting, not working class culture, but their own.

A more heterogeneous group waved the banner of a Revolutionary Eva at the time of my research. Because the militant Peronist Left was clandestine at this time, this group was not easy to define. A worker provided me with one of the most complete and coherent versions of this Eva's image that I was to encounter. Yet he and the few other workers with similar conviction whom I was able to contact recognized the influence on Revolutionary Peronism of new supporters, mainly intellectuals and members of the guerrilla—from the middle classes. These new Peronists, members of Peronist university organizations, trade union leaders, and participants in grass-roots groups of active militants, contributed to my formulation of this myth, though I had difficulty obtaining propaganda concerning the Revolutionary Eva from these informants and others.

Written sources have therefore been less important to my investigations into the Revolutionary Eva than to my research concerning the Lady of Hope and the Woman of the Black Myth. Analysis of this myth brought out certain parallels with the other two, suggesting that, wholly or in part, the Revolutionary Eva derives from middle class values, despite appearances to the contrary.

My research has not directly dealt with the acclaim that popular opinion abroad has accorded to the vision of the working class saint. But by questioning the origins of such an interpretation of Eva in Argentina, this work raises questions about stereotypes of women and of the working classes, which might account for the easy acceptance of the Lady of Hope elsewhere, even in serious accounts. [1]

The myth of Eva Perón thus confronts the anthropologist with special problems. Some complex industrialized societies which, like Argentina, have been relatively recently and rapidly constructed, manipulate symbols to provide an identity that externally or internally generated changes constantly challenge. The generation and transformation of symbols in response to wildly differing circumstances present special problems for the researcher. The absence in complex societies of a cohesive system of formal, traditional rituals dealing with defined types of situations contrasts with the relative unity of the symbolic universes of small-scale traditional societies, anthropology's classical area of investigation.

The consciousness of a need for symbols manifests itself in various ways. One of these is the rise of professional symbol makers. At another level, members of complex societies may consciously use traditional symbols to establish a cultural identity and to provide the illusion of continuity with the past in the face of changes radical enough to make a continuous identity virtually impossible. An anthropologist asks what kinds of contingencies give rise to the symbolic activity peculiar to such societies. One looks for the parallels and differences amongst situations that give rise to symbols, as well as amongst the symbols themselves. One considers the relative importance of social structural, psychological, environmental, demographic, and political conditions of symbolization. Relating these findings to small scale societies, one can illuminate the role of these factors in cases where they are obscured by the relative lack of change both in symbolic codes and in definitions of the occurrences to which they are relevant.

These general issues arise here. The myth of Eva Perón constitutes part of a series of cases that generated similar symbolism in response to a similar element in otherwise very different situations. Professional symbol makers were of central importance in forming Eva and her myth. At the same time, the figure of Eva Perón focused various themes in the symbolic histories of Argentina, in particular the attempts of different groups to create not South American, but European identities for themselves as the fully human bastions of civilization holding off the forces of brutish barbarism.

A woman who becomes as powerful as Eva Perón did, exciting so many lasting and varied myths, is rare. My first chapter begins to explain her lasting fascination by drawing attention to common ideas about the nature of women and to virtually universal symbolism concerning the position of women in society. These general considerations are followed in the second chapter by an outline, necessarily brief, of certain historical and cultural features that provide the background for the story of Eva Perón, indicating its complex relations to symbolic themes in Argentinian historiography. Next, the biography of Eva Perón is sketched. This documented version of her life is immediately contrasted with two major myths about her: the Lady of Hope of orthodox Peronism and the woman of the Black Myth of anti-Peronism. These apparently contrasting myths are analysed together in Chapter 5, which shows that they in fact share their underlying structure and values, and that these relate to the symbolism of female power. These symbolic patterns associated with the feminine nature of Eva Perón, then, yield significant parallels with imagery linked throughout Argentinian history with marginal sectors of society, the 'masses'. Finally, still another myth is introduced: that of the Revolutionary Eva, at first glance entirely different from the other two. Invoked by the Argentinian guerrilla forces and the militant Left, this Eva—both woman and revolutionary—displays characteristic elements of the imagery both of womanhood and of the masses. The conclusions to the study bring together the themes that have emerged concerning the relationship of feminine imagery with ideas of women's power.

Of the chapters that follow, only the biography and the first section of the historical background deal with historical fact as it is sometimes understood, that is, with 'what actually happened'. The rest of this book leaves this sort of fact behind and tells of mythic images. Where the myths have incorporated something that 'actually happened' these pages report it as part of the myths. The myths incorporate elements of 'reality' that contribute to their underlying pattern of values: others they omit. These elements are not included because they 'actually happened' but rather because they fit the myth: they become mythic. The case of Eva Perón reveals no easily perceptible point at which 'reality' ends and myth begins. These myths have used reality, and reality has been shaped by these myths. People have acted on what they believed to be the truth about Eva Perón, and they have acted as well on what they believed that other people believed about Eva Perón. They have acted on myths, and they have acted on a myth about those myths.

I

The Power of a Woman

Like Eva Perón in Argentina, other powerful women and powerful men in other complex societies have inspired popular enthusiasm which has in turn generated myths about them. But few have had comparable impact on the imagination of their countrymen: few peoples have enveloped their leaders in so many myths elaborated with such detail; few have continued to develop new personae for their heroes and heroines so long after they have disappeared from the national scene; few have found it natural that the myths and the bodily remains should play so important and active a part in official political manoeuvres as well as popular political allegiances.

Evita confronts us with the enigma of power attributed to a woman in a traditionally and formally patriarchal society, a society that devalues women as against men. Any attempt to solve this problem reveals another: how does Evita's power, as the woman's followers and enemies have conceived of it over the years, resemble attributes ascribed to women in positions of power in widely differing cultures, including both simple non-Western societies and modern Western states?

The myths of Eva Perón alone cannot offer definitive solutions to such problems. They cannot tell us precisely why the Argentinian First Lady was promoted and accepted in terms of imagery startlingly similar to that now surrounding Imelda Marcos, First Lady of the Philippines or that originally associated with Sirimao Bandaranaike, the wife and successor of the Prime Minister of Ceylon. Nor can they account for the similarity of the role of revolutionary attributed to Eva and that of another former actress, this time in China: Chiang Ch'ing, wife of Mao Tse-tung. We find no simple explanation of glimpses of parallel traits in portraits drawn by the American media of women such as Jacqueline Kennedy, during her husband's presidency the custodian of virtue in the form of beauty and culture, or Betty Ford, hailed as a spontaneously radical First Lady at the side of a comparatively conventional and conservative President. But from the mass of detail concerning the different images of Eva emerge suggestions that links may exist among these disparate cases of powerful women. Only by amassing similar detail concerning such women and others can these links be examined or new ones postulated.

In different formulations and different contexts, Argentinians have explicitly described Evita's leadership not as political, but as spiritual, moral or religious. At the time of her death Eva Perón was arguably the most powerful woman in the world. But Argentinians giving vent to their hatred or expressing their love of Eva Perón remember her special power as emotional and intuitive, violent, mystical, uninstitutionalized. To this, they add a particular emphasis: they describe Eva's leadership as irrational, unanalysable, uncontrollable. More than political authority, she exercised a sway, which according to varying versions of Peronism's propagandists and followers, was mystico-religious, moral, or spiritual.

Eva with her husband formed a ruling couple whose followers saw them as leaders with two complementary types of power. 'Perón *is* Peronist strategy', Argentinians say, 'but Eva *is* Peronist ideology'. Less often, Peronists repeated to me the old slogan of the first Peronist régime: 'Perón accomplishes; Evita dignifies [*Perón cumple; Evita dignifica*]'. Perón, some claimed, was the ultimate politician, while Eva could not be classified as a political phenomenon at all. The Peronist Left, which was at the time of my research beginning to merge with the Marxist Left, claimed that Evita was the 'spirit' of the struggle of the guerrilla resistance, while Perón himself was the 'content' of the fight. They fought with Perón's own tactics for his return, but Eva was the force behind the struggle.[1] In her autobiography she said that the difference between herself and her husband was that he was the one 'with the intelligence; I, with the heart', 'he, knowing well what he wanted to do; I only feeling it'.[2]

Was the imagery surrounding Eva fortuitous or does it suggest that she, and other women in similar situations or positions, provide images especially appropriate to a concept related to spiritual power? A close look at examples suggests that such symbolism may display a certain logic when it arises. In the early 1970s propaganda in the Philippines was lauding that nation's First Lady:

> Ferdinand would be the brain; Imelda would be the heart. Ferdinand would build the body; Imelda would provide it with a soul . . . As President of the Republic, Ferdinand E. Marcos concentrated on matters of state, peace and order, national unity, political and ideological conflicts, economic development and reforms, foreign affairs, education . . . His task was to build a nation, to weld all the diverse, clashing elements of Philippine society into one national homogeny . . . In the performance of that task he would likely be impersonal, even unsentimental . . . Men of power develop hearts of steel . . . They become inured to what Imelda has called 'the true and good and beautiful'. . . . She knew that the warrior President, in the implementation of his vision could neglect the finer aspect of life . . . Imelda would infuse the house that Ferdinand would build with goodness, truth, and beauty . . . The brain and leader of that unique revolution is Ferdinand E. Marcos; its heart—Imelda.[3]

Earlier, in terms that offer another example of imagery significantly similar to the Argentinian myths of Evita, followers of the newly elected Prime Minister of Ceylon, S. W. R. D. Bandaranaike,[4] had heralded his wife as a paragon of femininity. As such, this woman could act as the soul of the government, while her husband occupied himself with tactical concerns. Enthusiasts acclaimed her for her beauty and domesticity, admired her high social status, called her 'our mother', and described her as *sidevi*, possessing all positive traits attributable to womankind. As nurturant and bountiful, sympathetic and tender, Sirimao Bandaranaike personified the affective as against the instrumental aspects of her husband's regime.

After Bandaranaike's death, when the regime began to lose its initial popularity, the growing opposition blamed Mrs. Bandaranaike for the evils increasingly perceived in the government. She herself and her rule were damned in terms again linked with both her female nature and its implications of intuitive or instinctive power. When she first assumed her husband's office Mrs. Bandaranaike had appeared in partisans' descriptions as an honourable widow defending her husband's good name. Now, branding her as the cause of the difficulties of the régime and the nation, enemies emphasized the traditional definition of widows as inauspicious. Mrs. Bandaranaike had become *mudevi*, incarnating all the potential for evil inherent in femininity: her female sexuality uncontrolled, her maternal nurturance only feigned, she was seen as violent, vindictive, and irrational.

Not only such isolated cases, but the ethnographic literature in general, support the idea that the qualities thought to characterize the power of Eva Perón are linked both in Argentina and in other cultures with ideas concerning female power in general. An overview of concepts of power typically wielded by women suggests that they universally derive from a combination of several factors: woman's physical nature, involving her over time in the reproductive process as well as lactation; the social roles to which these physical conditions make it likely that woman be assigned; and the psychological concomitants of both.[5]

Both the precarious control which civilization exercises over her biological and sexual nature and her anomalous position in the interstices of society trap woman in an ambiguous state where she provides a major focus for central cultural ideas of purity and pollution.[6] Women are repeatedly defined in terms of the physical processes of which their bodies give such frequent and explicit evidence. These processes are seen as natural forces which must be kept within the limits set by the civilizing influence of men. Without necessary restrictions women become sources of pollution; carefully constrained by their culture's rules and regulations, they become important symbols of purity. At the same time, virtually all societies exclude women from their formal rankings and regulations, positions and goals, relegating them to the realm of domesticity outside official structures. The roles and power ascribed to women are informal and uninstitutionalized in contrast with the culturally legitimated statuses and authority attributed to men. Powerful or not, women and their behaviour are seen as 'idiosyncratic and irrational', ' "emotional" ', ' "happy-go-lucky" ', ' "spontaneous and confused" ', ' "affective" ', and ' "expressive" ', deviant or manipulative.[7]

From this context emerge three general types of sources of female power. Women may manipulate their domestic position, claiming loyalty, for example, as mothers, or offering or refusing performance of culinary, sexual, or other duties. Women may also manipulate the very symbols and ideology which limit their activities and set them apart from men, stressing the differences to their advantage. In this sense they can exert power over men, threatening them from the strength of roles as incarnations of evil and pollution, or, as incarnations of purity, keeping them at bay. Finally, women can, but seldom do, assume masculine roles, enter the world of men, and compete for power on the terms of the opposite sex.[8]

A cross-cultural perspective, then, reveals an association of women with the domestic sphere, a related general exclusion from institutionalized power, and imagery derivative from these conditions. This context renders it more likely that peoples both conceive of specific instances of women's power and portray them symbolically as spiritual, mystico-religious, or uninstitutionalized, rather than interpreting them as temporal, jural, or 'political'.

This thesis merits further consideration here because there is evidence that many cultures distinguish types of power, differentiating what might be recognized only as inherent analytical elements of a single phenomenon in other cultures. And in some cultures where types of power are distinguished, women are symbolically linked with a power similar to that of Eva Perón.

The appeal attributed to Eva, distinctly different from that of Juan Perón, directed my attention to this symbolic distinction elsewhere. Other ideologies distinguish political or temporal power, often institutionalizing it as complementary to another, spiritual authority. The two types of power may be distinguished and symbolized in various ways, according to differences in emphasis placed on each, or distribution of the two throughout social groups or institutions. In such cases as the symbolic relationship of the Gurage and Fuga of Ethiopia,[9] the Khans and Saints of the Swat Pathans,[10] or the Ksatrya and Brahmins of classical Hindu society,[11] temporal or jural power and spiritual or religious authority are attributed to different groups considered to have a complementary relationship.

If concepts of power or leadership often postulate a complementarity of different facets, there may be a certain logic in the assumption of spiritual leadership by the *wife* of a male political leader who can provide the other term necessary to the concept of total power. In this sense, a factor important in attributing spiritual power to women in this position may lie not only in imagery associated with the female sex, but also in the simple idea of the complementarity of the sexes. Societies may seize on any set of complementary relationships to use in symbolic statements of the duality of power. In this context, the interest does not actually lie in the content of the relationships other than their complementary structure. This makes possible the distinctive assignment of similarly differentiated facets of power to different complementary terms of whatever relationship used.

Nevertheless, and of more central interest here, there do exist cases that suggest that within a relationship between the sexes, concepts other than complementarity become highly relevant to the ascription of different powers to women and men. These concepts relate more directly to the nature of femininity or masculinity. The precise imagery surrounding Eva and her power and its parallels with conceptualizations of female power elsewhere indicate that there are certain contexts in which women are appropriate repositories of a certain kind of spiritual or mystico-religious power.

The case of Eva and Juan Perón, and perhaps the Marcos and Bandaranaike cases, seem to present a contrast of spiritual with temporal power, a formulation made in many different cultural contexts. These statements of the more generally encountered theme seem on the surface to make a simple association of femininity with spiritual power and masculinity with temporal power. However, as many cultures link men with spiritual authority, these husband-wife cases may be instances of a broader distinction: one between controlled power and uncontrolled power. Edmund Leach has drawn attention to such a contrast in his discussion of controlled supernatural attack and uncontrolled spiritual influence. [12] This opposition, too, can be subsumed in the distinction proposed here. Both attack and influence indicate power; and all power partakes in some way of the supernatural, the spiritual, the numinous, forging links with central cultural values. Institutionalized political authority, of course, is invariably a case of controlled power. But institutionalized spiritual authority may also represent a case of controlled power, contrasted with spiritual authority outside institutions and therefore beyond constraint.

I would suggest, then, that cases of a link between women or female traits and spiritual power may arise in a society's dealings with a spiritual realm partially or wholly beyond the bounds of its institutions and manipulations: a realm that is uninstitutionalized, uncontrolled, irrational or incomprehensible. An association might be expected between spiritual or mystic power of this sort and women and womanhood, characterized as intrinsically foreign to the rank and rationality of the formal social structure. On the other hand, when religious power is involved in social forms and control, societies might apportion this power to men.

Widely differing societies, including some Western ones, illustrate this association of complementary types of power with the two sexes. The symbiotic existence of the Gurage of Ethiopia with another group, the Fuga, drastically separates spiritual and political power. The ritual specialists are the scorned and dominated Fuga, who are politically controlled by Gurage men. The Fuga share a secret language with Gurage women. Further, in important contexts it is the Fuga *women* who are designated to fill the indispensable ritual roles.

By contrast, in a society where spiritual and political realms are together integrated into formal social structure and power, Hinduism's only classically sanctioned religious specialists are invariably male. However, women and other marginal groups do become specialists in popular, non-classical rituals such as exorcism, shamanistic practices, and personality cults. Hindu cosmology reiterates these themes of ritual practice. The priest, here the source of legitimacy or order, is associated with the male principle of the universe while the king is associated with the female principle and possesses a temporal power, which is deadly when uncontrolled.[13] The female principle embodies both active power and undifferentiated matter in the universe. The male principle, by contrast, is inactive and identified with differentiated spirit, structured or codified existence.

Females, and female deities, present the constant threat that their structureless power will slip out of control and become a malevolent force. In the absence of male authority, often that of a consort, it is felt that woman can loose mindless destruction and violence on the world about her. But her power can become benevolent when, as in myths of properly chaste wives who transfer their power to their husbands to secure victory for them in battle, she submits her power to men's control.[14]

In the Mapuche Indian culture of Southern Chile, the ritual priest (invariably a lineage elder, usually an elder of a dominant lineage, and ideally a chief) contrasts with the shaman, the machi. The priest operates in the context of a body of defined ritual lore and deals with equally defined kinship rights and obligations, extended to the ritual congregation, including the ancestors of participating groups. The shaman manipulates spirit familiars, becoming possessed by them, and is subject to attack by evil spirits. The priest, 'who does not grapple with the forces of evil directly', and who is integrated into the formal structures of authority of Mapuche society, is always a man. The *machi* or shaman whose different power is called upon in *formal* rites only 'where chieftainship or ritual skills are weakening', is always a woman.[15]

In Western culture, where concepts of institutionalized spiritual authority and uncontrolled spiritual powers have co-existed, the former has been restricted to men. The attribution of institutionalized spiritual authority to women continues to spark controversy and schism. But traditionally, spiritual power beyond institutional or even social control, has been imputed to, or exercised by, women—as in the case of witches, or, perhaps, of the wives of powerful men.

Western cases in which uncontrolled spiritual powers have fallen into male hands may have arisen when there has been no woman on the scene to whom they could be attributed. The widespread images of Fidel Castro as politician and Che Guevara as mystical leader of revolution might be examples of this. The death of 'el Che' emerges as another possible element in this popular version of the Cuban leaders, and will be discussed later in Chapter 8.

The nature of the association between women and uncontrolled spiritual powers, which appears in many cases in the ethnographic record, may vary with other features of social organization. There are indications that the more firmly a group relegates women to their place outside structures of powers and production, the more unambiguously it may associate women with uncontrolled or spiritual power. Studies concerning Mapuche society and South Indian groups showing widows as witches and as the perpetrators of random, apparently senseless murders by poison respectively bear out this suggestion. Amongst the Mapuche, those most often suspected of witchcraft are old women bereft of a solid position in society, most especially women who have married into their husbands' lineages and have survived not only their husbands but many of their children.[16]

Relative to other castes, the Havik Brahmins of South India give their women status notably more peripheral to social position and production. In contrast with Brahmin women, women in lower castes may own land, work in the fields or for wages, and engage in financial transactions independently of their husbands. Significantly, it is the Brahmins who most earnestly pursue menstrual tabus that identify women as a source of dangerous pollution, and it is they alone who fear their widows as the sources of random violence through murder by poison.[17]

In the West such considerations may be closely linked to social class. Studies of North American society show that, as middle class women lost their importance in home production, they occupied an increasingly marginal position within society and were correspondingly defined in terms not of societally legitimated authority but of spiritual, instinctive 'influence' exercised mainly by virtue of the exalted tutelary role of motherhood. This quintessential feminine power depended on an emotional, intuitive, unintellectual womanly nature which rendered women closer than men to the realm of the divine.[18] This definition and associated values may have affected a feminine ideal in other sectors of society, but they could not have greatly modified a working class reality in which women needed to contribute to family income or even support families alone. Such thorough studies of social values intimately related to Protestantism of a particular era have not been extended to Roman Catholic South America, although investigations have been made that indicate that parallel segregation of the middle class woman from spheres of public office and production occurred in some areas with some similar effects on values.[19] The feminine imagery emerging from the studies of the North American middle classes offers striking parallels to that located in the middle classes of Roman Catholic Argentinian society. The myth of Eva Perón could suggest that factors of class weigh more heavily than those of religion in the development of this feminine ideal.

Another implication emerges from the virtually universal exclusion of women from legitimized authority, and from the descriptions of them as outside or unqualified to enter this realm of institutionalized power. It might be expected that revolutionary roles would be attributed to women in positions of leadership or prominence. Evita Perón was characterized at different times as a revolutionary, sometimes in contrast with her husband. Mao's wife, Chiang Ch'ing, has been seen in a similar light, which has caused first her glorification and then her downfall, after the Cultural Revolution of which she was the special sponsor.[20] The imagery surrounding Betty Ford in the United States offers parallel themes, as mentioned earlier. Limited as it is to the detailed study of one case, the present discussion can only tentatively introduce this consideration in the hope that it might be taken up in further systematic investigations into the images of other powerful women, or couples.

Nevertheless, the different facets of the single case of Eva Perón offer preliminary support for the ideas suggested here concerning a connection between feminine imagery, uncontrolled power, and revolutionary leadership. Two of the myths to be examined, the positive version of the régime and its middle class supporters and the negative version of the predominantly middle class opposition, stress Eva's success or failure in fulfilling the ideal of womanhood. The myths formulate this ideal in terms that are intricately linked with the qualification of this female leader's power as spiritual or mystic and beyond the control of protocol, rules, or reason itself. The third version, in which Eva figures as the incarnation of revolution in Argentina for followers of different political persuasions and social strata, more directly attributes Evita's importance to her spiritual leadership, but does not emphasize her nature as a member of the female sex. The myth of the revolutionary Eva does, however, define the qualities believed to render her power special in terms which are again congruent with the feminine ideal that appears in the other versions. The Lady of Hope, the woman of the Black Myth, and the Revolutionary Eva all contrast Eva's leadership with political power exercised within the parameters of institutions, laws, and the corrupting constraints of human nature. They very explicitly deposit this political power in the hands of her husband, Juan Perón.

2

The Backdrop

Eva Perón's followers perceived her life at its simplest, as a journey from rural interior Argentina to city life in the port of Buenos Aires, from the deprived lower classes to success and wealth. In all this her life was representative of the path traced in a less spectacular way by their own lives, and the dream of success that lured them to this particular road. Many Argentinians see the migration from the provinces to the capital, of which Eva and her followers were a part, beginning before Perón's rise and increasing during his years in power, as a last variation on a theme central to the Argentinian view of their own history: the confrontation between rural and urban Argentina, between the interior and the port, between America and Europe, between barbarism and civilization. According to many, Eva succeeded in overcoming her origins on the scorned side of this opposition by her capacity to identify with and use the dichotomy's valued terms and to value the terms that traditionally had been damned.

The vitality of two diametrically opposed interpretations of Argentinian history, each of which has both popular and academic expressions, can disconcert observers from nations with a relatively unified national history (or from the dominant sector responsible for unifying such nations). The average Argentinian realizes that his own general conception of the nation's history, however vague it may be, often contradicts the version held by many of his compatriots, both in broad outline and in detail. One version of Argentina's history takes the form of glorification of Juan Manuel de Rosas, glamorous nineteenth-century ruler and hero of the gauchos; the other major version takes the part of Rosas' enemies, principally Rivadavia, Mitre, and Sarmiento. Each interpretation has both popular and academic expressions. Conflicts about the proper interpretation arise not only in a limited academic sphere; they are important in the continual formation and re-formation of ethnic and political identities and in conflicts among groups already established. The Argentinians insert these issues in treatises, report on them in weekly news magazines, and scrawl slogans about them on walls. Groups in conflict on grounds other than interpretations of history often feel pressure to identify with one side of the controversy and will trace to nineteenth-century leaders their ideological and sometimes even physiological genealogy.

Complex factors established a gulf between two Argentinas—the interior and the littoral. Parts of the pampa and, more especially, the littoral, share with Buenos Aires the traits that differentiate the entire area from the rest of Argentina. But the simplified popular concept of this division sets the sophisticated and wealthy European-ized port, Buenos Aires, alone against the provinces, considered deprived and less civilized. The symbolic opposition has taken the form of divergent culturally determined versions of Argentinian history, or political genealogies. Before turning to these, this discussion will first examine their sources in contingent events and conditions, in the cultural values arising out of these events and conditions, and in related imagery. The values and imagery behind the different histories as well as the histories themselves played an important part in attempts of Eva and Juan Perón, their followers, and their enemies in their struggles to legitimize their ideas and actions.

Three eras of Argentinian history with the symbols each threw up around itself will occupy the attention of this work here and at other points in its exploration of the nature of the imagery surrounding Eva Perón. Each era represents very different social, economic, and political conditions at the same time that all made certain very similar symbolic statements about themselves, despite their differences. This introduction of these cases focuses on the different historical context of each example of similar imagery. The imagery itself and the many parallels each case offers to the others provide the focus of a detailed examination in a later chapter. This chapter, while concentrating on the vast differences amongst the three historical periods, points out that the very different sets of circumstances and conditions do display one similarity: an upsurge of popular devotion to a political figure. Such fervour and the fear of it as a source of power trigger a reaction in groups which distinguish themselves from what they perceive as the popular masses. The reaction has consisted of the rise of mythic images in the social sectors which oppose the popular agitation. Such images express the opposition's ideas of the popular leader, of his followers, and of the precise form supposed to be taken by widespread enthusiasm. But these ideas base themselves, not on the nature of the leader and the existing popular sentiment for him, but on values of the opposing groups, which define themselves as middle and upper class. They generate such images at a moment when they believe society's balance of power to be threatened. They see their position in that society, and therefore their identity itself, endangered.

TWO ARGENTINAS

The profound differences and even enmity between citizens of the Argentinian interior and the littoral have generated some of the most fundamental oppositions in symbolism and myth within Argentinian culture, and have served throughout the nation's history as the basis for political and social justification and insult. The original settlement of the River Plate began in the time of the Spanish vice-royalties, but the area was not to become a vice-royalty until late in the history of Spanish domination of the continent. Argentina's oldest city is not Buenos Aires, or any other port. The nation was settled from the West, not the East, as towns sprang up along the mule routes to the riches of the mines of Upper Peru. The first city in Argentina then, was the now obscure Santiago del Estero. From the relatively arid northwest region of the country, the city could not take advantage of the future fruits of the pampas or the ports that were to create Argentina's wealth. In 1580, three decades after the founding of Santiago del Estero, a successful settlement at Buenos Aires was established by an expedition from Asunción, future capital of Paraguay. Trade restrictions continued for another century to orient Argentinian towns in the interior towards Péru, and still another century passed before a customshouse was first established at Buenos Aires in 1779. At this time royal decree had finally ended the Panamá-Seville trade monopoly and permitted trade between Spain and various New World ports as well as among ports throughout the empire.

In the intervening period, isolated from traditionally hispanic societies of the interior, the Argentinian littoral began to develop the unique character which would later allow Argentinians to perceive within their nation Europe and South America in confrontation. The coastal settlement lacked, on the one hand, family traditions and class structure directly imported from Spain and, on the other, large indigenous masses to provide easily obtainable labour. These factors helped to form a distinct ethnic identity for the area of the Argentinian littoral, and combined with the natural orientation of a port city toward commerce to make Buenos Aires a relatively open society.

When its commerce became legal, the city entered a period of economic boom. Easy fortunes and increasing immigration exaggerated the original possibilities of social mobility and promoted the success of non-traditional enterprises. The burgeoning economy was based on commerce and livestock. Hides and salted meat went to foreign markets to be exchanged for goods for consumers in the Argentinian coastal region. Meanwhile, the economic activity in the port meant that the interests of the littoral gradually became further and further removed from those of the interior, where small farms and industries needed domestic markets for their products. In economic terms, then, as well as in terms of ethnic composition and social structure, the two Argentinas began to emerge in opposition before Independence in 1810.

After Independence, these economic conflicts became overtly political as well. The popular heroes and events of the time came to personify the terms of later conflict, down to the Peronist era and beyond. Bernardino Rivadavia, elected the first President of the republic, was forced to resign his office after the provinces rejected his constitution of 1826. Rivadavia's defeat was seen as the defeat of his vision of a future Argentina modelled on Europe, towards which his progressive measures in government and development had been directed. Argentina entered the period known as the Anarchy, which saw the rise of the montonero guerrilla troops, their caudillos, and finally of Juan Manuel de Rosas, who vaunted himself as the caudillo of caudillos, and eventually brought relative unity to the nation under his mid-century rule as governor, granted 'supreme and absolute powers'.

While Rosas' actual bases of power displayed contradictions and cannot be summed up simply, he claimed to represent, with the montoneros and their leaders, the true Argentina of the interior in its struggle for power with the effete Europeanized denizens of the capital. At this time, the main trade in salted meat from its *estancias* oriented Argentina away from Europe and towards the major slave markets in the New World. Rosas' later tariff barriers protecting the industries of the Argentine interior also directed the economy away from Europe. This was an era dominated by the large landed interests employing a relatively small labour force, mainly of itinerant mestizo gauchos. A typical hispanic stratification of society still existed, with the gap between upper and lower classes containing only a tiny middle class of around ten per cent of the population. The Federalist Party under Rosas represented the landed interests, but ostentatiously cultivated the support of the gauchos. At a time when the balance of power between the landowners and the commercial interests of the port was in question, the Argentinians who felt threatened by Rosas' solution to the problem saw him as a menace to the world as they knew it. Rosas' régime became in their minds an eruption of the forces of disorder rampant in the lower classes, which jeopardized the order of European civilization and the Argentinians' identity as Europeans.

This conflict of Rosas' Federalists with their progressive liberal enemies thus gave birth to an opposition which future Argentinians used as symbolic of other oppositions throughout their history. New developments inevitably were seen within this framework. The status of Buenos Aires as the nation's major contact with Europe, its control over the port revenues, its later central position in the railroad network, and the mushrooming of increasingly labour-intensive agriculture on the pampas, all continued to augment the power of the littoral after the fall of Rosas after the Battle of Caseros in 1852. This, in conjunction with massive immigrations from Europe, reaching a peak in the last twenty years of the nineteenth century, could only, in this context, eventually exacerbate the image of European civilization pitting itself against the hordes of the interior.

The flourishing economy of the city had drawn larger and larger numbers of foreigners until, near the turn of the century, more than half the people on the streets of the metropolis were foreign-born. The newcomers made it yet harder to preserve in Buenos Aires traces of traditional hispanic culture. In less than half a century they had redefined the *porteño*, or dweller of the port, with a wave of immigration consisting of more Italians than Spaniards, and a significant proportion of Eastern Europeans, Frenchmen, Englishmen, Germans and Arabs. They laid the basis for a present-day Argentina containing, in contrast with the stereotype of Latin American nations often held elsewhere, a highly Italianized culture, a large and important British sector, and the third largest Jewish community in the world, surpassed in size only by those in New York and Tel Aviv.

The Argentinian perceives this population of the capital and the littoral as ethnically and culturally distinct from that of the interior. Further, with the transformation of the composition of the population, the great immigration of the last half of the nineteenth century changed the social structure of this area, again accentuating the already apparent contrast with the interior.

The port, with its dependence on foreign trade, had always supported a relatively large commercial middle class, especially when compared with the traditionally hispanic society of the interior towns. As the *estancias* turned to modern cattle breeding, sheep raising, and the cultivation of cereals, the Argentinians under the government's *laissez faire* policy turned to export markets mainly in Europe. At the same time, for a variety of reasons, access to property was increasingly difficult for the many Europeans hoping to obtain land in the New World. Opportunities in Buenos Aires attracted growing numbers of immigrants. As trade boomed and urbanization increased, the numbers of the middle class grew to forty per cent of the population, many contributing to the formation of a predominantly dependent economic sector as they administered the growing foreign capital that overwhelmingly dominated the nation's economy.

The members of this sector contributed importantly to the identity of the burgeoning Argentinian middle class. They did not see themselves as an independent bourgeoisie proud of pulling themselves up by their bootstraps. Dependent on an economy dominated by upper class and international interests, they found an important model for their values in those of Argentinian and European upper classes.

Conditions in Buenos Aires were such that dreams of social mobility could be realized often enough to perpetuate them. The flux of Argentinian society exacerbated conditions that would become chronic problems on the Argentinian scene. The promise of ascent to groups on higher levels of society magnetized the attention and energy of the Argentinians, impeding the creation of solidarity or a sense of identity within groups temporarily on their way up the social ladder. Added to this, the massive immigration smashed the illusion of a mainstream 'Argentinian' identity to which new arrivals could adapt. Recent arrivals and a continuing involvement in domestic economies or national conflicts in Europe constantly renewed the foreign identity of the resident groups. Social aspirations and widely varied ethnic identities conspired to create the social fragmentation and political factionalism that have characterized the splintered Argentinian reality since that time.

The prosperity of the 1880s, when Buenos Aires had dressed herself in French ideology and architecture, was followed by a short recession and yet another boom, which caused fortunes and hopes of fortunes to flourish. Rising expectations instigated violent protests against acts or circumstances that threatened to limit ambitions.

Radicalism too was on the rise. Essentially a middle class movement, it counted on small farmers, tenant farmers, shopkeepers, and white-collar workers, with support from the urban working classes formed by tradesmen and others from the Old World. These workers were not only educated, but also versed in the ideologies and modes of labour organization in Europe. Argentina soon had the largest organized labour force in Latin America. But this organized labour force was concentrated in Buenos Aires, its members and its ideologies representing predominantly European traditions. Basically, since all depended on the export economy, the interests of these middle and working class sectors coincided with those of the large landholders: confrontations emerged over the redistribution of profits. Nevertheless, again in the midst of flux, Argentinians attempting to preserve tradition or status perceived such confrontations as endangering established positions in an established order of things. And once again, for those who felt threatened, the danger took the form of masses blindly following a leader, this time, Hipólito Yrigoyen, who at the turn of the century was a caudillo of growing importance in the Radical movement. Yrigoyen's Radicals, it was thought, would array themselves as forces against order—any order: they would attempt to extinguish civilization itself.

Later, after the Depression of the 1930s, the Argentinian world tottered yet again. Transformations in world markets had made industrialization increasingly necessary at the same time that these very conditions kept such a goal always just out of reach. The polarization of Argentinian society in the face of continuing disintegration of its structure of power has continued into the present. These conditions set the scene for the rise of Eva Perón, the person and the myth.

The middle classes have felt the threats of such a situation more and more acutely. Because many middle-class sectors have been economically dependent and have traditionally espoused upper class values, the identity of the middle classes has remained ambiguous and insecure in a special way. Many feel themselves to be above not only the working class, but much of the lower middle class as well. Yet in the context of the continually deteriorating economic situation of Argentina, which in recent years has displayed the world's highest rate of inflation and a precipitous decline in real wages, the line of demarcation between lower and middle class groups has become less and less distinct. Meanwhile, the middle classes are not accepted by the upper classes. In this uncertain position, many of them attempt to maintain a symbolic distance from the groups they define as lower classes in order to establish claims to an equally symbolic proximity to the Argentinian aristocracy. This they do by defining themselves in terms of values they believe to characterize the upper classes in particular and mainstream European civilization in general. From this definition they explicitly exclude the working classes by designating them as diametrically opposed to its terms.

Because the boundaries of the middle classes are indefinite and therefore are manipulated according to the aspirations of different people or groups, the concept itself operates as an important symbolic construct in Argentinian culture. The resulting flexible definition of the Argentinian middle class, current within Argentinian society itself, will be the only one used throughout the present study.

The stereotype of the Peronist movement has been one of a working class party consisting predominantly of *cabecitas negras*, the uneducated immigrants from the interior. As Argentina's economic power, and with it foreign immigration, began to decline a new kind of immigrant began to arrive in the capital, attracted from the provinces to the centre of the nation's life. The *porteño* who defined himself as middle class perceived these arrivals as more than provincials: he saw them as a race of which he had been unaware in his own country.

The nature of the immigrants and their origins have been investigated in the literature exploring the phenomenon of Peronism, but of greater importance here is the salience of stereotypical beliefs about them. The new arrivals in Buenos Aires are believed to have been a race apart, uncouth, uncivilized, with a liability to demagogy and violence, the seeds of a primitive loyalty to Juan and Eva Perón. In the increasing uncertainty of Argentinian society the new masses, like other masses at other moments seemed to menace annihilation of Argentinian identity as it had been understood until that moment.

The middle classes have sought refuge from this threat in anti-Peronism. The identification of the middle classes with anti-Peronism had been so complete before the recent second Peronist regime, 1973–1976, that those who were Peronists generally rationalized their position with special formulations to demonstrate that, in terms of their middle class social status, they actually belonged with anti-Peronism or were the social equals of anti-Peronists. They attempted to establish symbolic identity with not one but two groups: they desired the status of the middle and upper classes while they needed the support of the masses. Because of this, the positive image of Eva Perón contains a direct statement of the same values found in the negative anti-Peronist image, but Peronists who hold this image identify it as the belief of the masses. In their eyes it reflects the fanatical adoration which the Lady of Hope inspired in her working class following. This version, then, includes important parts of an essentially negative image of the masses current in anti-Peronism, but imbues them with a different value. It exalts them as virtues of the popular following of Perón. This allowed middle class Peronists to link themselves with working class Peronism without identifying completely with it. Meanwhile the image of Eva Perón, which these middle class groups promoted, with its inclusion of important status symbols, laid their claim to a social and cultural level equal to that of the anti-Peronist middle and upper classes.

The followers of the Revolutionary Eva just before the second Peronist regime identified themselves completely with the masses. While it is possible that not all members of this militant sector were of middle class origin, it was heavily influenced by that class and gave rise to an image of Eva's working class army similar to the image of the masses in other middle class myths, both the positive and negative versions. Members of the Peronist Left at the service of Eva abandoned the status symbols of the Lady of Hope. But they pledged themselves to the Revolutionary Eva, affirming that both she and they formed part of a mass movement which was both spontaneous and intuitive. Because she displayed the same qualities, they placed Eva at the head of this movement.

Others besides middle class Peronists evinced deep ambivalences about their political positions. Middle class anti-Peronists seemed to feel that they had to account for their affiliation to the anti-Peronist coalition. Certain factors complicated their situation, including areas of Peronist policy which directly benefited the middle classes as well as the uncertainty of the middle classes' relationship to the upper classes, also anti-Peronist. The rationalizations of middle class anti-Peronism, commonly very emotional in nature, were often made solely in terms of the images of the Peronist First Lady.

In all these cases the images of Eva Perón are quintessential symbolic statements of the cultural values at play in a choice of political allegiance that constitutes a claim to cultural identity.

TWO POLITICAL GENEALOGIES

Many different groups claim to monopolize Argentinian patriotic values, a claim they justify on the same grounds: that they have inherited them from the Liberator, San Martín, to the Argentinians the greatest of the heroes in the struggles against Spanish colonial rule. Throughout the campaign of 1945, the anti-Peronists attempted to expose Peronists as the carriers of the violence, according to his opponents, that Rosas had spread throughout Argentina, branding his regime as The Terror. Only the anti-Peronist coalition, said its members, could save the true values of San Martín. When Perón won the election, Eva Perón exulted in her husband's possession of the 'seat of Rivadavia',[1] while Peronists declared that it was no accident that this throne had been won by the greatest majority in the department of Caseros, a name which brings to every Argentinian mind the scene of the final defeat of Rosas. The Peronists thus demanded recognition of a popular mandate bestowing on them the legacy of San Martín kept safe by the enemies of Rosas. Perón himself apparently still identified with the opponents of Rosas, and encouraged such identification, when he renamed railroad lines newly purchased from Great Britain after Urquiza, Mitre, Sarmiento, and Roca, politicians who bitterly opposed Rosas, as well as San Martín and Belgrano, heroes of all Argentinians.

Peronists and anti-Peronists waged this battle over the possession of the family tree of patriotism, postulating clear-cut political and historical traditions deriving from the confrontation between Rosas and his enemies, and between the different Argentinas which they represented. This encouraged the idea that there had in fact existed not only two contrasting or even opposed cultural areas in Argentina, but also that each had given rise to a continuous historical reality and political genealogy contrasting and often opposing those of the others.

This may be an illusion arising from the political conditions of the Peronist era. The original revisionist statement of Argentinian history, which examined the role of Rosas and his politics, responded to certain conditions in Argentina in the 1930s and expressed a rejection of political tendencies of the régime consolidating the revolution of the beginning of that decade. In particular it protested the apparent favour with which the government treated foreign interests as well as a failure to unite the nation in the face of the gap believed to be widening between the élite and the masses. In the face of similar problems, the early revisionists held, Rosas had taken a strong nationalist stand and had united 'all social elements'.[2]

This early revisionism, then, emphasized factors that corresponded to the issues of the day. Since that time, different groups, responding to different needs and crises, have emphasized new elements separately or added them to the original formulation, increasing political fragmentation. But only in the dramatic confrontation of social sectors generated by the Peronist and post-Peronist years did these varying statements crystallize into full myths, seen as tradition, incorporating many of the earlier interpretations. Although new splinter groups continued to evolve, there was a predominant impression of an opposition between two 'traditions', ultimately made up of all these elements from throughout the past four decades and only in the last twenty years seen as wholes.

The two formulations can be traced back to the long-standing conflicts that culminated in Rosas' rise to power, his defeat by Urquiza, and the suppression of provincial uprisings during the presidencies of Mitre and Sarmiento. The Argentinians who opposed and finally defeated Rosas and those who, nearly a century later, subsequently claimed them as political forebears, harked back to his rival Rivadavia, as their link with San Martín. The ideals of Europeanization as well as of independence and liberal democracy flowed down this line from the Liberator to the future through the figure of Saenz Peña, the member of the conservative oligarchy responsible for the law establishing the secret ballot.

The contest for legitimacy in these terms, then, takes the form of the attempts of conflicting groups to graft themselves onto the line descending from the founding fathers, while attributing to their enemies roots which they believe to be cursed or blighted. But the dispute can take another form. Some groups have opted to declare the orthodox tradition a bastard lineage and to recognize its opposite as legitimate. San Martín had bestowed his sword on Rosas, a gesture exalted as acknowledging the Federalist leader, not his opponents, as legitimate heir.

This version sees the Liberator passing down the values of nationalist independence and denying those of European liberal democracy. The montoneros and their caudillos were hailed as the defenders of this tradition, both in the War of Independence and in the uprisings following the fall of Rosas. It was they who carried the ideals symbolized by the sword of San Martín safely into the twentieth century, when they were taken up by Yrigoyen and his popular Radicalism. Argentinians have formulated Yrigoyen's link with Rosas and thus ultimately with San Martín as more than symbolic: although it is fading in the minds of modern Argentinians, belief still survives in the legend that Yrigoyen himself was an illegitimate son of Rosas.

Adherents of each version of the history must necessarily condemn those who advocate the other by construing negatively the events and personages exalted by the enemy group. When the Peronists identified their original electoral victory with the battle of Caseros, they were immediately associating their opposition with Rosas and his troops, the villains of the orthodox version of the event. Anti-Peronists used the same tactic to discredit Peronism, by declaring Perón's fall in 1955 the 'Second Caseros' deposing the 'Second Tyranny'. They had employed this negative symbolism before: drawing parallels between Perón and Rosas, between their wives, Eva and Encarnación, and beween the mass followings of these two women, to denigrate Peronism.

It may have been only after the Peronist movement was definitively placed on the margins of power that Peronists began firmly to assert a positive association with the figure of Rosas. Many maintain this link today. It is no accident that when the second Peronist régime in the 1970s brought back the embalmed body of Eva Perón to a final resting place in Argentina, plans were made to return the remains of Rosas, who had been buried in exile in England, to his homeland as well.

Argentinians involved in the struggle for the coveted inheritance of San Martín have disputed more than a political stand. Their claims and counter-claims concern their rights to define themselves as civilized beings, and, beyond this, as human rather than primitive and even animal. An important expression of this was Sarmiento's masterpiece, *Facundo*, a classic of the Spanish-speaking world as a whole and which, familiar to every school child, still figures in the Argentinian mentality more than a century after it was published. *Facundo* was named after Facundo Quiroga, powerful caudillo of the Argentinian interior, and was likened to Rosas. The author subtitled the work *Civilization and Barbarism*. Here he claimed the definition of civilization for the European liberal intellectual tradition, which he represented, and hurled the insult of barbarism across the Andes at his enemy Rosas' régime and its adherents. This formulation still plays a key part in attempts at discrediting a person or group by association with Rosas, clearly showing the issues at stake to be more than formally political. Its terms will echo throughout this study of the myths of Eva Perón and related imagery, manifesting in the full context of Argentinian culture their connotations of a contrast between the dignity of the human condition and depraved animality.

Sarmiento's *barbarie*, familiar to most Argentinians and formulated here as nearly as possible in the words of Sarmiento himself, is a mode of life of an entire people represented by Facundo Quiroga: Argentina's indigenous barbarism in confrontation with European civilization. Barbarism means the absence of intelligence, of science, of calculating reason.[3] It negates, while civilization confirms, art, education, the 'elegance of manners', the 'comforts of luxury'. Poncho-clad, barbarism is the antithesis of culture, which might be symbolized in the European tailcoat—a style associated with Christianity, civilization, and the 'renaissance of the sciences'.[4] *Barbarie*, ignorant, superstitious, instinctive, dominates through violence, terror, brute force.[5] It resembles a force of the nature that engenders it and within which it thrives. Facundo, 'the man of nature who has not yet learned to contain or disguise his passions, shows them forth in all their energy and delivers himself to all their impetuousity'.[6] 'Quiroga . . . was barbaric, mean, lascivious.'[7] 'And in spite of all this, Facundo is not cruel, is not bloody; he is a barbarian, no more, who does not know how to contain his passions which, once they are aroused, know neither restraint nor measure'.[8]

This opposition between civilization and barbarism appears re-peatedly in different forms in the imagery surrounding and related to Eva Perón. Again and again the context will re-affirm the con-clusion that the dichotomy does not represent a contrast between political opinions or parties but that it identifies such contrasts with a gap much wider: that which separates humanity from the subhu-man.

3

The Biography

On May 7, 1919, an Indian midwife helped an unwed mother give birth to a child on the Argentinian pampas near the small town of Los Toldos, in the province of Buenos Aires. This child was to be Eva Perón, First Lady of her country and at the height of her career perhaps the most powerful woman anywhere in the world. But at birth Eva had no claim to the name Perón, nor even to the name Duarte, which she would use in the following years. She was Eva María Ibarguren, illegitimate child of Juana Ibarguren. Her father, Juan Duarte, denied her his surname.

In 1926 Duarte died. Two mothers of his children mourned him, his mistress, Juana, and his wife, the sister of the mayor of the city of Chivilcoy. Duarte had cultivated his contacts with the Conservative party as well as with the local landowners, making himself a respectable and prestigious neighbour. By renting fairly large extensions of land, he had prospered, finally becoming known as an *estanciero*, or landowner, an indication of status sought by many Argentinians more avidly than the actual possession of land itself.

Six-year-old Eva arrived at her father's wake accompanied by her mother and her four older siblings, all illegitimate children of Duarte. The society of Chivilcoy had also turned out to pay respects to the brother-in-law of their mayor. This gathering of upright citizens suddenly found itself the arena of a violent confrontation between the family of the deceased's wife and that of his concubine. The legitimate daughters publicly barred the entry of the second family. A quarrel broke out and continued, neither side conceding ground, until the mayor himself finally intervened, allowing the outcasts a last glimpse of lover and father and the privilege of accompanying the coffin to the cemetery.

To a child plagued by scandal, life in any pampa town offered little alleviation of shame or insecurity. When she was twelve, Eva, her mother, sisters, and brother moved to Junín, a larger city of over 20,000 near Los Toldos. People in such towns, behind the ornate little grey facades and their sidewalks, or in formal plazas displaying stiffly pruned trees, still seek isolated sparks of interest in the misfortunes and rivalries of their neighbours. Intrigues of the characters of popular radio programmes and, later, films, while increasingly occupying attention, have never replaced the staple gossip. 'Small town, large hell', say the Argentinians.

So Eva may have dreamed of escape from Junín and painful memories. But, like other young people, she probably hoped to leave behind the pampas themselves: here the towns, which in their formality and sobriety seem minute cities, also seem even more peculiarly lifeless than the slowest, most rustic village elsewhere. Sons and daughters of the local merchants, professionals, and civil servants plan futures in the big city. The landowning classes, although sometimes owning a residence in the town nearest their ranch, bypass it when distance permits in their usual trajectory from 'camp' to capital. Personal and financial investment in these centres has always tended to be minimal: they are way stations for people and products en route to the port. The proximity of Buenos Aires magnetizes dreams, ideas, and the people themselves.

At fifteen, in an Argentina feeling the repercussions of the Great Depression, Eva left her family and made her way to the capital city. Under adverse conditions, with the theatre in a crisis of competition with the increasingly popular cinema, the thin, dark child from the provinces found her way about one of the world's largest cities stalking her dream of a career as an actress. For ten years, a time when her frailty and occasional hunger worried better known members of the theatre world, her hunt was grim and silent, and its trophies tiny. But amongst them, by the time she was twenty, were radio parts. To a young actress at the time, these held the promise of a growing audience, burgeoning popularity, and, finally, with luck, a contract in national cinema.

In 1943, Eva Duarte's luck was holding. She signed contracts for the title roles of a new radio series announced as 'Famous Women'.

At twenty-four, the skinny, dark, little provincial was heard by the nation as a radiant, blonde Elizabeth I, as Catherine the Great, as Alexandra of Russia, as Carlotta of Mexico, as Sarah Bernhardt. The creator of these new Evas, Francisco Muñoz Azpiri, moved quietly behind his series of glittering successes. He was never to emerge from the background. But neither did he disappear from the life of Evita Duarte until well after she had added to her roles of Famous Women that of Eva Perón.

It was the popular actress of these roles who attracted the most rapidly rising figure of the new military government, Colonel Juan Domingo Perón, in early 1944. When the dashing Perón at forty-nine met and formed a liaison with this actress of half his age, his influential backing immediately made itself felt in moulding his protegée's career. Eva Duarte was soon acting in a new radio adventure series and began to prepare several cinema roles.

'She gives the impression of being on her guard', declared the magazine *Radiolandia* at the height of Eva's new wave of activity and popularity. 'The fact is that no actress recently has been the centre of so much rumour in her profession.' Eva, attempting to explode some of these rumours in an interview, in her anger instead put the substance of the tales on record, denying that her wardrobe was excessively flamboyant and repeating a public statement concerning the sources of her finances.[1]

During this time, Muñoz Azpiri, whose Famous Women she continued to portray, was creating a new kind of role for her as heroine of the government in which Perón's power continued to grow. Soon after meeting Perón, Eva had introduced him to the librettist, whose nationalist political convictions had made him a supporter of Perón. Within weeks, Muñoz Azpiri was Director of Propaganda in the state Subsecretariat of Information.[2] For half an hour three times a week, 'Towards a Better Future' offered the public dramatic definitions of Evita Duarte: 'Here is the voice of a woman of the people—she herself of the anonymous masses—in whose voice has been revealed day by day the nature . . . of this saving revolution'. When Eva herself spoke, she proclaimed, 'I am a woman like you, mothers, wives, sweethearts, sisters. . . . From me came the son who is in the barracks . . . or the worker who is creating a new Argentina in the land, sea, and air'.[3]

Eva seemed bent on assuming this role away from radio microphones, although she had not essayed this type of activity before knowing Perón. The Secretariat of Labour and Welfare, one of Perón's major bases of power and popularity which had been created less than a year before their meeting, confirmed the twenty-five-year-old actress in her first union activities, recognizing her as head of the Asociación Radial Argentina. This association, in conflict with others attempting to organize radio employees, received official authorization to act as their sole representative. Eva Duarte also, at Perón's request, occupied a small office in the Secretariat itself, without salary or conditions of any sort.[4]

Meanwhile, she did not neglect her earlier radio public. As her programmes continued, she addressed her audience in an open letter:

> Friends: The link of so many months with the microphone of LR3 Radio Belgrano must necessarily have created in us by now the special relationship of friends. The fact is, we are friends, and we are such with that type of friendship which is generated by the shared enjoyment of something emotional and moving: The characters which I interpret on the air . . . What more can I say about myself which has not already been amply treated in the press? . . . in an almost childlike way I live and dream each of the characters which I act. I actually cry over my strange, fascinating destinies . . . With this fresh and sincere voice I would like to proclaim how loyal I am to all of you . . . it hurts me to think that I do not reach your hearts. . . . My greatest satisfaction—as a woman and as an actress—would be to offer my hand to all those who carry inside them the flame of faith in something or in someone and in those who harbor a hope: . . . Friends [*amigas*], I have closed another chapter of my confidences, and I hope that it has not reached you in vain, knowing that in Evita Duarte exists your best friend.[5]

In early October, 1945, both Eva Duarte and Juan Perón seemed to have reached the height of their popularity and activity. Suddenly, on October 9, the increasingly vociferous opponents of the military régime and of Perón's growing power forced this champion of the workers from the Secretariat of Labour and Welfare to renounce the three government offices which he had by this time taken over: Secretary of Labour, Minister of War, and Vice-President. Only slightly later her radio employers fired Eva Duarte, and without Perón's backing power her post in government disappeared.

Perón's military colleagues themselves had considered the openness of the Vice-President's relationship with Eva and her presence with him in military quarters as continuing affronts to their respected traditions. Eva's occupation of a position in a government dependency in Labour and Welfare infuriated the military further with the suspicion that she influenced Perón's ideas. With dramatic disregard of this tension, the government had passed over the armed forces' candidate for the post of Secretary of Communications to appoint a known friend of the Duarte family instead.

Five days later the couple fled Buenos Aires in search of refuge in the delta islands near Buenos Aires. The police intercepted them on the night of October 12, conducting both back to the city. Then Perón entered exile alone aboard a gunship heading for Martín García Island.

From his island prison Perón wrote Eva long letters possibly intended more for his enemies, through whose channels he had to send them, than for Eva herself. Fearful of the outcome of his situation, he railed at the treachery responsible for it. If only all ended well, he promised, the only ambition he had would be to leave the false friends and loyalties of politics behind, marry, and return to his native Patagonia for a family life in isolation and tranquillity.[6]

No one has yet discovered what Eva thought or did while Perón was writing these letters. Abandoned in Buenos Aires, she had taken refuge in the house of a fellow actress. In the increasingly agitated climate of the city, a gang on the street recognized her in a taxi. Shouting 'It's Evita, boys, we've got to give it to her'! the men pulled her out of the car and beat her. Perhaps Evita was waiting, hoping against hope that the promises of the love letters could somehow be realized. Perhaps she found her ideas changing as she watched, with the astonishment of the rest of the giant city, a completely spontaneous workers' protest forming itself into the most powerful demonstration of its kind yet known in the history of Argentina. Perhaps, although evidence here consists only of claims and counter-claims of different factions of the workers' movement, she not only waited and watched but participated in the uprising as well.

Labour leaders had set for October 18 the general strike which was to protest Perón's exile. But the workers, ignoring the pre-arranged strategy, set out from their factories and marched unexpectedly on the centre of the capital on October 17. Columns of men in work clothes, not the suits usually demanded by the city of Buenos Aires, poured through the streets leading to the Plaza de Mayo's formal fountains, lawns, and palms in front of the Pink House of government.

The numbers and appearance of these crowds in shirtsleeves appalled many of the inhabitants of the city centre, who were glimpsing for the first time another Argentina, a brown-skinned mass that threatened the most prized identity of the *porteño*, his assured definition of himself as European. The intruders waited in the plaza, chanting Perón's name, sitting on the grass, wading in the fountains. Some carried for the first time banners proclaiming 'Perón for President'.

For those who watched the invasion with fear, the dispersion of the demonstration brought little comfort: the *'descamisados'* or 'shirtless ones', as they were to be known, had not gone away until they got what they wanted. Perón had appeared before them and had embraced the other members of the government on the balcony overlooking the patient crowds that had unremittingly demanded his return for long hours of the hot spring day. Five days later he married Eva Duarte, but, far from returning to the Patagonian steppes, they together launched his campaign for the presidency of the nation.

In early 1946, Argentina's fairest elections to that date made Juan Domingo Perón President. For the first time in the history of the nation, a wife had accompanied a presidential candidate on his campaign tours. Key to the campaign as a principle director of propaganda was Muñoz Azpiri, who followed Evita when she left his radio dramas to join her husband in his crusade for the presidency. Later, as she rose to power, he continued to write speeches for his star, now the First Lady of the Republic.

The new wife of the President claimed her new authority as the right of a First Lady. But this was a right never before exercised by the spouses of Argentinian presidents. No woman had ever assumed the title in so official a manner. Attacks rained down on the presumption of a mere starlet of radio drama and cinema. Since the position which she had attained had been previously no more than honorific, it was up to Eva to define it as something more. At twenty-seven, she set out to do so on the basis of a year in Labour and Welfare and no formal experience.

Did Eva prepare herself or was she prepared for power? It seems incontrovertible that she now moved to lay the bases for power: a power which she did not live to arrogate as her own or to share with Perón. Muñoz Azpiri was still at her side. A woman also accompanied the new President's wife in this period: Isabel Ernst was Labour Secretary to the Presidency of the Nation, formerly private secretary to popular Colonel Domingo Mercante in the Department of Direct Social Action in Labour and Welfare. Perhaps Ernst could impart enough of her own experience to her quick pupil so that the novice Eva could soon fill eighteen hours a day in what was now the Ministry of Labour and Welfare. And, of course, there was Perón, who was to claim until his death that he had prepared Eva and made her everything she was.

Even before Perón's election Eva began to deliver speeches, at first on her husband's behalf, but very soon on her own. The audience at her initial attempt, wanting no substitute for the candidate they had hoped to see and hear, shouted their protests, the clamour drowning out the birth of one of the most effective rhetorical styles ever known in South America.[7] Less than a year later, in December 1946, when Perón was in office, Eva set out by train for Tucumán, the seat of the sugar industry in the north, to be crowned Queen of Labour. For the first time, Perón stayed behind, although Isabel Ernst continued to accompany Eva. This time she was not shouted down. The surge of the crowd at the arrival of the new First Lady left nine dead and many more hurt.

Meanwhile, both Peronism and its enemies gradually focused a spotlight on María Eva Duarte de Perón. This woman, known only in Argentina, whose last publicity notice as a radio actress had appeared at Christmas 1945, had involved herself before Christmas 1946 in all the complex roles which would make her a political figure of international importance in only six years. Thrilled or alarmed, Argentinians watched Eva's growing contacts with organized labour, her activities in social welfare, her feminist initiatives, and her influence in the press.

Eva had begun to build experience in the area of labour, which Perón himself had made important, very early in their relationship. She continued her efforts after his election to the presidency, gradually taking over her husband's role as patron of the Argentinian worker. But although she was named the First Worker of Argentina in July of 1946, and Queen of Labour in November, Evita and the press made clear for two more years that she and her popularity were totally and unconditionally identified with Perón. In this capacity she began touring factories. A little later, although she was not yet identified with Labour and Welfare as she would be in future, Eva began to receive workers' delegations on her own.[8] As soon as early

1947, she was meeting with twenty-six labour delegations in one day. At this time diplomats and government officials had joined unions. The stream of the innumerable poor with their individual problems that had begun to flow through her office continued over the years to become one of the traditions most firmly associated with the image of the young blonde woman who received homage and dispensed favours seated at her desk.

When her husband took office, Eva had probably expected, as all wives of presidents had before her, the traditional invitation of Argentina's exclusive charity, the *Sociedad de Beneficiencia*, to preside as its president. But the invitation never came. Eva, the society let it be known, was too young for such a position. Eva sarcastically responded that perhaps her mother would do. The Executive Power took control over the aristocratic organization in September, 1946, and Eva Perón established an office in the building her enemies had vacated. She had begun to prepare the way for the expansion of her own nascent social work into the spectacular multi-million-dollar *Fundación Eva Perón*.

She, or the powers behind her, removed impediments to her growing influence in other areas in a similar manner. Before her first year in the presidential residence was out, she had formed and headed a Women's Suffrage Association (*Asociación Pro-Sufragio Feminino*) and was delivering weekly speeches on Peronist feminism. The official press backed her efforts, although not yet explicitly, in a series of articles dealing with women's problems in general and their claims to civil rights.[9] At the same time, she began to organize grass roots activity amongst women by creating feminist civic centres (*entidades cívicas feministas*) throughout the city of Buenos Aires and the provinces. But when other Peronists attempted to jump on this bandwagon, whether out of sincere conviction or hoping to use it as a base for their own power, Eva reacted with definitive antagonism. In early 1947, a message from the Secretary of Labour to the Presidency stated flatly, according to the anti-Peronist press,

> Referring to the reiterated denouncements received in this secretariat, according to which persons foreign to the same are invoking unduly the name of Señora María Eva Duarte de Perón in order to effect activities of a proselytic nature in centres and civic feminist organizations, among which persons are Doctora Longoni, Señorita María Luisa Raina and Señora Frugoni: neither these persons nor any others are authorized to invoke the name of the wife of the President of the

nation in this respect or in any other; nor do the persons named maintain any relation or contact with Señora Perón or with this secretariat.[10]

A similar report appearing around the same time claimed that when the wife of the Governor of Córdoba created a Centro 'María Eva Duarte de Perón' devoted to the ends of the First Lady's 'civic campaign', Eva responded by creating a rival centre and announcing that the registers were open in both.[11]

Her activities in all these areas—labour, social aid, and feminism—echoed increasingly throughout the media while Eva began to inject her influence into positions of authority responsible for communications as well as into strategic organs themselves. By January 1947 she had bought the newspaper *Democracia*, and her praises filled the first edition displaying a new format. This paper, now her property and perhaps her instrument and mouthpiece, bestowed on Eva (already First Worker, First Samaritan, and Queen of Labour of her nation) the new title of the Lady of Hope [*La Dama de la Esperanza*]. Having originally depicted the Lady of Hope as emerging from a spontaneous baptism of Eva Perón by popular Peronism, *Democracia* more than a year later admitted in a printed editor's comment that 'In pure truth, it was precisely here, in *Democracia*, where Señora Perón was justly called 'La Dama de la Esperanza', fitting epithet which is today on the lips of millions of beings'.[12] *Democracia* continued a spectacular campaign throughout the following year, during which all the Argentinian daily papers, with varying degrees of enthusiasm and elaboration, found themselves publishing news releases on the activities of the wife of the President in almost every edition.

How far did the power of this neophyte politician extend, only one year after her transformation from actress into First Lady? Her own press and other organs supporting her husband's régime de-emphasized any possible example of an initiative on her part, while her enemies seized upon similar examples to paint her as a threatening and dominant force in government. The fears of her opponents, although possibly exaggerated, may with equal possibility represent perceptions of otherwise undocumented influence, which Eva had begun to exercise in a significant number of areas. Her adversaries accused her of interference in congress, in the labour unions, and in national policy making; of giving instructions to governors, legislators, and government officials; of controlling the economic life of the nation; and of imposing her ideas in the universities as well as in the school system. [13]

In June 1947 Eva took a step thought by those who dreaded her growing consequence and magnetism to confirm all their fears. She had accepted an invitation of Franco to visit Spain, and now prepared to depart on a voyage perceived by the contemporary opposition as inextricably involved in a drive for further power. Anti-Peronists were unable to dismiss the tour, as did many later, as a mere personal satisfaction for a social climber, permitting her to establish a new bourgeois identity in order to compete with her enemies in Argentinian high society. Eva flew to Madrid from Buenos Aires, for the Argentinian navy had denied her a ship for the voyage. Her enemies saw the impending tour as a further usurpation of official functions and prerogatives.

The Peróns defined the tour as unofficial, Eva herself claiming that she was financing it with her own funds for the purpose of informing the Old World of the peace, stability, favourable labour conditions, and optimism in the New Argentina. [14] Yet the regime allowed Eva an entourage and the power to sign certain official agreements with European governments. Lilian Guardo, the friend whom Evita chose to accompany her during the tour, later remarked that her companion telephoned Buenos Aires twice daily, one call to Perón and one to the National Congress: 'There she mobilized all the ministers and officials who were waiting for her call, from whom she demanded details of the government and to whom she gave specific orders'. [15]

The drama and semi-official nature of the tour possibly served the interests of Franco and both Peróns. Franco, soon to be isolated by the United States and the Marshall Plan, needed a promise of aid and a demonstration of alliance from South America's most powerful nation. Perón needed to define his own relations with the United States, in the face of criticism from nationalist groups, both Peronist and Radical, of his position in the Interamerican Conference on Problems of War and Peace in Chapultepec, Mexico City. Perón may have hoped that his friendly gestures toward the Spanish government, then being ignored by the United States, coupled with a delay of the ratification of the Acts of Chapultepec, would convince his critics of his independent position. Eva herself was acting in the context of the steps she had already taken toward creating a powerful role and image for herself that had little resemblance to the Argentinian ideal of the wife of the President of the nation. Her official visits and impressive public receptions contributed to her image of a classic socially acceptable President's wife, but they further underlined a new phenomenon: her ability to share and even wield the power of the President.

Members of the Radical Party of the opposition lodged protests in Congress itself. The question of the justification of sending a priest and military aides-de-camp to accompany Eva on a supposedly unofficial visit arose, stirring animosity. Radical representative Ernesto Sammartino spoke up to propose a law refusing any wife of public, private, or military officials a share in the honours or privileges of her husband. He proceeded to mention a peculiar similarity between the illicit enjoyment of official prerogative which he had just condemned and 'the present tour of the President's wife'. The phrase, unfinished, threw Congress into chaos and forced the session to close. The violent reaction to Sammartino appears in the incomplete record disproportionate to the offensiveness of his proposal itself. It might indicate that this was an occasion for some of the deputy's famed public invective against the Peronists and their leaders, such as his comparison of Argentina to a cart stuck in the mud and pulled by a mare.[16]

The exuberant twenty-eight-year-old blonde took in her stride the cheering farewells of 500,000 Argentinians and the welcome of the ruler of Spain, the 'motherland', and 300,000 Spaniards. Franco bestowed upon her the honour of the Cross of Isabel the Catholic, while Eva in turn promised the gift of a shipload of wheat to the Spanish nation. After a series of enthusiastic receptions all over Spain, she continued to Italy. A bomb placed in the Argentinian embassy before her arrival and demonstrations outside her lodgings, which became shouted protests against the Fascism of Perón and Franco, marred her stay in Rome.

On June 27, Pope Pius XII received the First Lady of Argentina. Although a papal decoration arrived at the Argentinian embassy for President Perón during Eva's visit, the Pope granted her no honours other than the customary rosary bestowed as a token of an audience. Shortly after this encounter, exhaustion forced her to break her schedule in order to rest, at doctor's orders, for her last days in Italy.

Next on her itinerary was a long-anticipated visit to Great Britain. This trip had absorbed the attention of the Argentinian and the

English press and public since its announcement. Different groups in England, variously interpreted the aims of the visit as commercial or military, involving purchases of material for the Argentinian navy or air force. Even as Argentinian newspapers claimed that their 'Presidenta' was to be a guest of the royal family at home in London, English reports made clear that such a visit would be neither proper nor desirable. [17] For a nation emerging from war against Fascism, the First Lady of a régime labelled as Fascist arriving after a triumphal visit to a Fascist régime was likely to be unpopular. To the delight of the anti-Peronist press, the Royal Family announced that they planned to be in Scotland at the time of Eva's visit and therefore could not receive her. Eva's enemies interpreted this to be a judgement of Eva as a socially undesirable guest. Officially, the controversial journey was never made because of Eva's 'state of prostration'.

From Italy, she continued to Portugal and then on to France. In Paris the Minister of Foreign Relations, Georges Bidault, met her. She lunched with the French President, Vincent Auriol, and later signed a treaty that granted France an Argentinian loan for the purchase of wheat and meat.

Eva was met with open acts of hostility in Switzerland. She was pelted with vegetables, and a recent immigrant, an Argentinian of Swiss descent, threw stones at her car, breaking the back window. Cartoons of Eva with tomatoes splotching her clothes subsequently appeared in anti-Peronist papers in Argentina. The caricatures marked the last issue of many of these newspapers, amongst them the eminent Radical *El Intransigente* of Salta and the Socialist *La Vanguardia* of Buenos Aires, immediately closed by the Peronist régime. Still later, Perón's investigators claimed to have discovered that the shower of tomatoes had been instigated by the wife of the heir to the famous Bemberg fortune in Argentina, which was heavily fined on other grounds. The fine itself went to the Eva Perón Foundation. [18]

From Switzerland, Eva travelled to Lisbon to embark on the sea journey home, as ordered by her doctor in a last attempt to force his patient to rest. In Rio de Janeiro, a special session of the Chamber of Deputies received her. She lunched with Brazil's President, Erico Gaspar Dutra, and attended the current Conference of American Ministers. The conference reserved her a special seat behind the Argentinian delegation and further honoured her with an intermission, champagne, and presentation to the ministers.

Shortly afterward, jubilant Peronists saw their Evita fall into the arms of her husband, who met her ship by launch in the port of Buenos Aires, on August 23 1947. The Eva in the photographs of Perón's welcoming embrace no longer displayed the elaborate curls and falls of blonde hair, the plump figure, and the flamboyant clothes and hats of the Eva who had left her country for Europe. Hatless, she had combed her hair austerely back, beginning a change to the streamlined, eternally classic style that she made uniquely hers until her death. She continued to dress for the role of '*compañera*' of the poor and the workers of her country, frequently and gracefully appearing as she had from the beginning, in sweaters and skirts, slacks or simple cotton dresses, often with her hair tucked up under a scarf. She continued as well to take advantage of her more feminine and extravagant glamour, which she used for formal occasions and in summer dresses until her death. But after her return from Europe, these images were increasingly complemented by a sober and elegant Eva clad in tailored suits.

Within months of her arrival from Europe, Eva had consolidated the position for which she had laid the base before her triumphal tour, as her trip was remembered amongst her followers. In order to increase her power from this point onwards, she had only to run the elaborate machinery she had created or that others had created for her. She appears to have employed the year between mid-1948 and mid-1949 to build on the foundations she had laid. Gradually she extended her virtual control over three and perhaps four important sources of power: the feminine branch of the Peronist Party, her Foundation of Social Aid, several of the most important organs of the official press and possibly labour as well. With her importance in these areas, her influence increased dramatically in politics within the government itself. By the middle of 1949, Eva had established the role that would characterize her until her death, with the exception of only a few minor new undertakings. In this period she began to use the shortened form of her name, signing and identifying herself no longer as María Eva Duarte de Perón but as Eva Perón.[19]

Shortly after the return of the First Lady to her country, the Chamber of Deputies granted women's suffrage. Mass assemblies of women celebrated the event, accompanied by a spectacular fanfare of publicity. Days later, the Superior Council of the Peronist Party moved to change the structure of its organization. The motion opened the way for the creation of the Peronist Women's Party and, for Evita to assume, two years later, leadership of this powerful branch of Peronism.

By mid-1949, further changes completed the institutionalization of Eva's leadership of Peronist women. Eva met with the Peronist Superior Council, definitively restructuring the Peronist Party, making room for a feminine branch independent from masculine sectors. Within four days of the formation of the Peronist Women's Party, its grateful members made Eva Perón their president by popular acclaim. In the following months and at the elections, this party contributed to the nation female deputies and senators as well as the world's first female congressional president.

A decision to minister to the unfortunate of the world at large as well as the poor of her own nation heralded the burgeoning of Eva's social aid campaign. November 1947 saw her first shipment of goods for charity abroad as well as, significantly, the beginning of the end for aid in post-war Europe from other Argentinian charities.[20] By the early months of 1948, Eva was completing a housing project in the province of Buenos Aires. She installed drinking water in areas of Córdoba, carried out innovations in the National Direction of Minors (*Dirección Nacional de Menores*), and inaugurated her first Transitional Home for women immigrants from the interior. The First Lady's plans for a children's city, a cross between an educational model and an amusement park, were underway when, on April 14, she received the title of 'Spiritual Mother of All Argentinian Children'.[21]

The recognition of the María Eva Duarte de Perón Foundation of Social Aid as a corporate legal entity came in June 1948. It was to be staffed and administered by the Minister of Finance. Eva herself personally contributed 10,000 pesos (in 1948 equivalent to $2,500) to the organization. The Executive Power made arrangements for a budget that was later to become a source of fierce controversy: initially it was to come from two days' wages subtracted from the annual salaries of all workers and employees as well as from all extra funds in the budgets of other ministries. Within five months of its inauguration, the foundation's capital increased to 23,000 pesos. This amount more than quintupled in one year. Between 1949 and 1952 the budget increased from 122 million to 2 billion pesos. During 1949, the Chamber of Deputies voted an additional 70 million pesos for the foundation's budget, but Perón himself vetoed the bill. The Minister of Finance, Antonio Cafiero, later approved this action: 'We did not need those 70 million . . . Perón was right in doing that; it was not right that the legislators wanted to make a good impression on the Señora at the cost of the national budget'.[22]

Its enemies had levelled bitter criticisms at the foundation, and continued to do so. The anti-Peronists resented the elimination of the traditional and aristocratic Sociedad de Beneficiencia. The Peronists justified Evita's suppression of the society on the grounds that its efforts had been nothing more than charity to ease the upper-class consciences and to provide good excuses for fund-raising balls. The anti-Peronists answered that the foundation was also only charity and that it was aimed towards obtaining votes, despite its claims to be administering 'social justice'. They declared that the foundation was responsible not only for the loss of the Sociedad de Beneficienca, but for the decline of various private institutions in the interior as well, as they lacked funds formerly allocated to them by the National Congress.[23]

The harshest accusations against the Eva Perón Foundation have concerned its finances. Over and above the obligatory contributions established by executive decree, the Foundation received voluntary donations from individuals, unions, and other groups, including business enterprises. Although the contemporary Peronist press gave a great deal of publicity and importance to the private voluntary contributions, Ramon Cereijo, former Minister of Finance and Administrator and General Agent of the Foundation, claimed later that 'The majority of those who personally brought an important donation came only to be photographed with the Señora; they did it purely to polish apples or to exploit their pretended connections with the government'. However, the anti-Peronists affirm that the Señora carried out a large part of her social aid with money belonging to other people and institutions, and that she extorted these funds under threat of personal or financial disaster. The most frequently cited examples of this treatment are the closing down of the Mu-Mu candy company and the Massone pharmaceutical laboratories. These cases have never been clarified, although Cereijo rejected the accusations as unfounded: 'Why would we do that when we had all that we needed? The financial support of the two-workday contribution was enough for us'.[24]

The Foundation's work proceeded with two new Transitional

Homes, vacation colonies for working class children, and plans for a first home for the elderly. Over the following years hundreds of thousands of small soccer enthusiasts all over the country underwent medical examinations for the first time and put on their first pairs of shoes and socks in order to play in the Juvenile Championship tournament created by Eva and her advisers.

During 1949 the projects of the María Eva Duarte de Perón Social Aid Foundation took on mammoth proportions. Eva inaugurated the storybook Children's City for her Argentinian charges, while continuing her contributions to the unfortunate in other nations. She made a generous donation to the poor of Washington, D.C., thus causing some consternation in the United States. By this time the efforts of the First Lady were choking out parallel endeavours of other Argentinian private organizations and public figures. As it continued to grow in the following months and years, the foundation dominated public health and education, almost replacing the ministries ordinarily responsible for these areas. Nurses' schools, homes for students and 'student cities', more vacation colonies, clinics for convalescent children, modern hospitals, and a thousand schools went up around the country. Later, in 1951, when Argentina was suffering increasing inflation, the organization, known officially since 1950 as the Eva Perón Foundation, established a chain of supply houses to dispense basic necessities at controlled prices in limited income areas.

These activities kept the First Lady constantly before the eyes of the nation. Her publicity served to form her image along certain lines, consistently veiling other areas in which evidence suggests that Eva was active and important. For the sake of the credibility of their praises of her activities elsewhere, the régime and its organs did not publicize Eva's movements within the realm of official propaganda itself. The story of Eva and Peronist propaganda still consists only of fragments. Her influence in the press began with her purchase of *Democracia*, which rapidly became the most important government mouthpiece. But her further association with other periodicals is less definitively established, although Argentinians often refer to her alleged control or ownership of the papers *El Líder* and *El Laborista*.

The radio librettist Francisco Muñoz Azpiri, who was originally linked with Eva, had participated actively in early stages of the Peronist movement during the period of establishing the general lines of the images which both Eva and her husband were to follow throughout their careers. His part in defining these images remains obscure, but his work in the early propaganda of radio's 'Towards a Better Future' and his importance as Director of Propaganda in the Subsecretariat of Information show that he actively participated in creating the régime's propaganda. He continued to write speeches for Eva, the star of his early radio dramas, until after her tour of Europe, on which he accompanied her. Later he drifted off into oblivion, apparently because of conflicts within the Peronist Party.

Raúl Apold, who later held Muñoz Azpiri's title in the Subsecretariat of Information, became an important figure in *Democracia* with its purchase by Eva Perón. The influence which Apold wielded from the Subsecretariat illuminates the importance of the more modest Muñoz Azpiri's position. The power of the office grew in the years between Apold's appointment and Eva's death as it took over control of the editorial line followed by the nation's most important newspapers. The régime silenced others which did not follow this line, with the exception of *La Nación*, which was muted.

Another friend of the First Lady, Major Carlos Vicente Aloé, found himself in charge of the periodicals being brought under the régime's control. When the Peronists purchased in early 1949 the majority of shares in the Editorial Haynes, publishers of ten periodicals, Eva personally requested Aloé to place himself at the head of the enterprise despite his protests that he knew nothing about publishing. He also became president of the board of directors of Alea, S. A., a concern that printed almost all the publications that followed the official line.

Although this picture of Eva's role in the propaganda that swathed the Peronist movement and government is incomplete, there are suggestions that her influence amounted to virtual control. They point not only to the First Lady's importance in the area of the official press, but to the fact that she had established as well significant personal contacts and friendships with three crucial shapers of Peronist propaganda in general: Muñoz Azpiri, Apold, and Aloé.

Official coverage downplayed not only Eva's role in the press and propaganda but also her action and influence in labour and in the party and its government.

The régime had enthusiastically and increasingly identified Evita with labour since her early days as First Lady. During her husband's first two years in power, however, when the press described her contacts with the labour movement as part of her social work, her role as patroness of the workers apparently involved little, if any, open political action on her part. In 1948 this began to change. In early March Juan Perón named his wife president of the Third International Congress of Social Security held in Buenos Aires. Two weeks later Evita intervened openly for the first time in a union conflict when she received the credit for solving a problem for some bank employees, though the media did not record the details of her role. From this point onward, the official press referred constantly to Eva's participation in the solution of different labour problems, while seldom giving any details of the exact nature of her intervention or its outcome.

In 1951, the newsvendors' union launched an offensive against *La Prensa*, one of the most important newspapers of the opposition. Its demands on behalf of the employees of the paper for a rise in salary as well as one-fifth of the advertising revenue received official government support, and *La Prensa* was expropriated. The régime's position in itself might have implied support from Eva or possibly even an active role in the solution of the problem. But when *La Prensa* changed hands from its former owners to the labour syndicate centre, the CGT (Confederación General de Trabajo or General Confederation of Labour), Eva made her participation explicit: she herself presented the wages lost by the workers during the closure, paid by the funds of the Eva Perón Foundation.[25]

During the same year the Peróns confronted one of the most serious of the labour protests made during their years in power, and the only one with recorded overtones of protest against Eva herself and her policies in labour affairs. The railway workers had declared themselves on strike on November 24, 1950. A strong group of Eva's followers had controlled the Executive Committee of the Unión Ferroviaria as well as the position of Secretary General of the union which was held by Pablo López, a favourite of the First Lady, and discontent with this state of affairs had triggered the strike.[26] To the usual 'Long live Perón' on signs and walls, some of the protesters made an addition of one word: 'widowed'.[27]

Eva openly assumed an active role in the attempts to solve the railway dispute. Not only did she carry out her usual negotiations with the union delegations; she tried as well to persuade the strikers directly, appearing sometimes at midnight or later to speak to them where they were gathered in the train stations. The bureaucratic hierarchy apparently regarded these attempts with ambivalence, if the vacillating interpretations of the official press were caused by pressures from those spheres of power. In mid-January, the press reported that Eva had participated in making important concessions to the Co-operative of Personnel of State Railways. During this period, the newspaper of the Unión Ferroviaria, *El Obrero Ferroviario*, perhaps in response to the bias in favour of Eva in the union's official ranks, stressed Eva Perón's role over her husband's in the solution of the strike.[28] Eva's actions, however, had no appreciable effect on the strike, which was ended after a series of more drastic measures on the part of the government.[29] Meanwhile, throughout these events, the press had first designated Señora Perón as arbitrator in the problem and then, in an official retraction of this report, called her a 'permanent friend' helping through 'friendly mediation'.[30]

Only later, as Eva neared her death, did the press include slightly more detail concerning her role in labour affairs. Reports included vague references to a meeting of the secretariat of the CGT at which Eva Perón presided, as well as to weekly meetings with labour leaders held by Juan and Eva Perón together in the Casa Rosada. These muted indications of the real extent of Eva's influence in labour affairs may support the conclusion that she had come to manage all governmental agencies dealing with labour and exercised responsibility for contracts, pensions, collective bargaining and all disputes.[31]

An increase in her recognized importance in the Peronist government and party paralleled the development of the role of Eva Perón in all other fields of activity. She made numerous tours of the provinces, all of which the contemporary press noted in detail. But in other areas her action, as in the case of her intervention in the field of labour relations, was informally and badly documented if it was documented at all. The year of 1948 apparently included some frustrations or errors as Eva continued the task of creating her unique role. But by mid-1949, Evita Perón seemed to have established the political identity which was to remain with her for the rest of her short life.

Eva's behaviour at the beginning of 1949 offered a striking contrast with the role she was to adopt as that year went by. In January, the First Lady was invited to speak at the Constitutional Convention about to be held. But she declined, according to the official press, stating that she only interpreted her husband's ideas. She never again refused to speak on the grounds that her place was that of a mere interpreter for her husband.

The new official position which Eva occupied in the Superior Council of the Peronist Party as a result of the informal and enthusiastic endorsement of Peronist women of Eva as president of the Feminine Branch of Peronism meant a more independent and institutionalized role for her within her husband's party. At the same time, her personal influence over members of the government itself, outside the official definitions of her position in the party, gave her an important source of power.

Aside from any weight her opinion had in the decisions of her husband, Eva's unofficial influence in the government may have begun as her relatives were appointed to positions of varying importance. During the first years of the Peronist régime, the opposition uneasily repeated accusations of nepotism, indicating the rise of the 'Duarte group' in different offices. One of the most impressive of these rapid ascents was that of Eva's brother Juan, who obtained a post through the new First Lady as inspector of the Casino of Mar del Plata. Just a year and a half later, Juan Duarte moved into the office of private secretary to the President of the nation. His sisters and their husbands had risen from various obscure posts to fill the posts of Inspectress of Postal Savings, directress of the National Normal School, national senator for the province of Buenos Aires, member of the Supreme Court, and head of customs for the port of Buenos Aires.[32]

Later Eva extended her government influence far beyond family ties. By 1950, according to some, Eva had all but created the Cabinet that was appointed in the middle of that year. One such report alleged that the First Lady had caused Perón to replace the Minister of Agriculture, the Secretary of Technical Affairs [*Asuntos Técnicos*], the Minister of Industry and Commerce, the Minister of Finance, the Minister of Education, and the Minister of Foreign Relations. It is widely known that the last two of these cabinet members, Minister of Education Ivaníssevich and Minister of Foreign Relations Bramuglia, did not enjoy the favour of Eva Perón. The replaced Minister of Finance remained in the government only when others prevailed upon Eva to create a new ministry, Economic Affairs. Eva herself, according to the same report, notified some of the men who had lost their positions in her husband's cabinet. In addition, Ricardo Güardo, at the time the President of Congress, states that Eva sometimes called on him to arrange a gathering of 'her' ministers at the same time as scheduled Cabinet meetings. Those ministers who met with the First Lady, then, arrived so late to Cabinet that the military ministers had already retired. [33]

Eva's influence in foreign affairs may have gone further than her alleged intervention in the dismissal of Bramuglia from the Cabinet: foreign observers, writing while Peronist government was still in power, remarked that Eva and her friends played a role greater than that of any minister of foreign relations and equal to that of Perón in defining Argentinian foreign policy. [34]

In mid-1950, only a year and a half after she had excluded herself or had been excluded from the Constitutional Convention, Eva played a notable part in the first Conference of Governors of the provinces of the nation. In the time between the two events, her position seems to have changed and her power increased to such an extent that no longer could the word of Eva Perón be omitted, nor would she herself offer to decline an invitation. [35] If this interpretation of her presence at the first Conference of Governors is correct, it offers an intriguing and significant contrast with the version given in the official press. Not until the events of the following year, amongst them the Second Governors' Conference, does the Peronist press begin to suggest that Eva may have been acting as a political power in her own right. [36]

The way her popular following view any development in Eva Perón's character and role provides an indispensable context for the interpretation of these changes. The Peronist working classes may perceive some transformations in Eva during her career leading to her assumption of responsibilities and an identity different from those of Perón. But they place the changes and differences within the larger frame of the continuity of co-operation and the complementary nature of the Peróns' relationship, while this in turn is subordinated to the dominant mind and overall strategy of Juan Perón.

Such ideas qualify speculation that the trend towards a transformation of Eva Perón into a political figure in her own right and with her own character might have indicated a growing independence from Juan Perón or even a conflict between the two. Whether or not Eva had thoughts of making herself independent of her husband or of his particular ideology would be relevant only if she had lived to realize her hopes or if the people had supported her as a figure separate from that of Juan Perón, representing different ideas or goals. Neither of these conditions took place. Nor did she ever, despite the fears expressed by the contemporary press of the opposition, seem to have usurped any part of Juan Perón's position or support. Rather, the two would seem to have touched different chords of popular response. [37]

Neither Eva nor Juan Perón ever lessened the stress they placed on Eva's identity as intermediary, as the 'bridge of love' between Perón and his people. Perón himself formulated his version of this role long after Eva's death:

> One of the greatest forces of women in leadership is that they use the little means [*pequeños medios*] which are so powerful, something which we do not do because we are men. They take advantage of this, and one should see the strength they have! This must undoubtedly be a factor of strength which women offer us in politics, a factor of extraordinary strength. [38]

> Eva Perón is an instrument of my creation. I prepared her so that she would do what she did. I needed her in the sector of social work within my leadership. And her work was extraordinary ... My life at her side formed part as well of the art of leadership. As a politician I am barely an amateur. The area in which I am a professional is in leadership. A leader must imitate nature, or God. If God came down every day to solve men's problems, we would already have lost our respect for him and there would be no lack of some fool who would want to replace him. For that reason, God works through Providence. That was the role which Eva filled: that of Providence. [39]

Eva also, in her book and her speeches, emphasized constantly the dual nature of her relation to Perón: she not only fused her being with that of her husband, but she also could approach him as part of, and identified with, her people. She had become part of Perón through her love for him as his wife, and through his magnanimous gesture of loving her, choosing her amongst all her fellow 'descamisados'. But she had been born 'descamisada', and while Perón remained forever unique, Eva's identity was collective: she did not only champion the humble; Eva *was* her people.

Eva's ascent was not, as it may sometimes have seemed, entirely without limits. At different times during her years of increasing power, Evita confronted opposition from enemies within government itself. For example, the antipathy between Eva and Bramuglia arose at the beginning of their acquaintance, apparently due to a basic conflict of personalities or purposes, when Eva unsuccessfully sought a writ of habeas corpus from him for the exiled Juan Perón in 1945. Although Eva possibly, as some accounts claim,[40] exercised key pressure to prevent Bramuglia from becoming governor of the province of Buenos Aires in the early years of the Perón régime, she was unable until much later to eliminate him from the Cabinet altogether.

Eva may also have felt she needed to contend with old friends who showed signs of too much popularity in the very sectors where the First Lady herself was hoping for supremacy. Her efforts could have ended the careers of labour leaders Luis Gay and Cipriano Reyes, the latter denounced as the author of a plot against both Peróns in September, 1948. She possibly involved herself as well when Domingo Mercante was relegated to the sidelines. A companion of the early days of the régime, he was so popular that he was considered a possible candidate for the vice-presidency instead of Eva.[41]

Meanwhile the military's resentment of Eva's influence over Perón remained unchanged from the days before their marriage. The Armed Forces complained adamantly about the increasing activity of the First Lady, even, according to one version, turning her away from the gate of the Campo de Mayo, a central army base, when Eva tried to make a surprise visit in 1949.[42] But neither the complaints nor specific pressures which the military might have brought to bear appear to have affected Evita's role until, perhaps, very late in her career. Tension between the armed forces and the First Lady may have come close to the surface in Eva's attempt to arm the Peronist workers in 1951. From her sickbed Eva apparently was able to negotiate the purchase of 5,000 automatic pistols and 1,500 machine guns, using funds of her Social Aid Foundation. The abortive uprising against Perón by General Menéndez may have inspired Eva in this action, as the purchase was made shortly thereafter, on September 29, 1951. She communicated her decision secretly to José Espejo, Secretary General of the CGT, to Isaías Santín and Florencio Soto of the National Secretariat of the same organization, and to General José Humberto Sosa Molina, commander-in-chief of the army. The ailing Eva bought the arms through Prince Bernard of Holland, and they were delivered on April 15, 1952.

Eva planned to establish workers' militia to defend Perón and

Peronism. She succeeded in having such groups actually set up, according to some Peronists who cite names of various men put in charge of them. They participated in manoeuvres with the armed forces until pressure from the latter forced Perón to dissolve the new groups. These Peronist versions claim that the army became alarmed by the efficiency and skill of the worker soldiers. Other accounts state that the arms were never used and that Perón first stored them in the Arsenal Esteban de Luca and later sent them to the Gendarmería Nacional.[43] The plan may have evinced a new trend of thought and action in the life of Eva Perón; some Peronists as well as others of the Argentinian Left laud it as such. Eva, however, did not live long enough to be able to indicate the real significance of her act.

What effect differing enmities and influences had on Eva's career cannot be more than guessed. Another check on her power, and finally her life, ended both before the others could make definitive marks: Eva Perón was fatally ill.

Since her days as a radio actress, Evita's delicate health had forced her periodically to take prolonged periods of rest. Her increasingly frenetic activity made these intervals of rest shorter, despite the pleas of the doctors attending her during the European tour and afterward. On January 9, 1950, in the midst of a public ceremony in the hot summer sun, Evita Perón fainted. Her doctor, Oscar Ivaníssevich, also Minister of Education, insisted on a full examination during which he made note of inexplicable pelvic pains, swelling ankles, a persistent fever, and vaginal haemorrhages. Her symptoms had made sexual relations impossible since the previous year. Ivaníssevich recommended an immediate hysterectomy.

The operation, performed on January 12, and the short convalescence following it, concluded the incident. But in retrospect it would seem to have marked the beginning of a superposition of themes that characterized Eva's last years—and perhaps most of her life. One of these was the anticipation of her own martyrdom for the sake of the Peronist cause. Another was her apparently staunch refusal to take any course of action other than that of fatal self-sacrifice. A third was her defiant insistence, in the face of the destiny she was forming for herself, on increasing her activity to levels that would have been sustained with difficulty even by a healthy person.

Well before there was any evidence of the extent to which her health actually had been undermined, Eva had set the scene for the event so that when it occurred its explanation had already been made. 'I will give my all', she announced in a speech one year before her collapse:[44]

> I left my dreams by the wayside in order to watch over the dreams of others, I exhausted my physical forces in order to revive the forces of my vanquished brother. My soul knows it, my body has felt it. I now place my soul at the side of the soul of my people. I offer them all my energies so that my body may be a bridge erected toward the happiness of all. Pass over it . . . toward the supreme destiny of the new fatherland.

Eva must have known early that she was draining her physical resources to an extent that could only be damaging and perhaps very dangerous. But she consistently refused to do anything to reverse the process or even to retard it. Despite the urgency with which Ivanís-sevich recommended the hysterectomy, Eva stubbornly resisted. When her husband intervened, demanding that she undergo the operation, she did so. But upon recuperating she plunged anew into a schedule so arduous that Ivaníssevich was led to protest. On the occasion of one of his remonstrances, Eva, oddly furious, slapped the minister across the face. Ivaníssevich resigned his position less than a week later, on May 18, 1950.[45] He himself has stated that the reasons for this resignation lay in his perception of the growing corruption in Perón's régime.[46]

What could have motivated Eva to behave in this manner? Some have suggested that she suspected the men around her of attempting to use her illness as an excuse to curtail her political activity. Others claim that she could not believe that her power could be limited by a factor so petty and arbitrary as her health, or that she did not know how sick she really was.[47] The nature of her cancer, however, and the length of time she must have been aware of disquieting symptoms before their diagnosis, should be considered as well. Women in such cases are often inordinately late in consulting a doctor about their symptoms. Eva may have been desperately sure of her doom.

Whatever personal reasons Eva may have had for her attitude toward her physical condition, she provided the media responsible for publicizing her activities with one of their most important themes in reporting the events of the last years of her life, even before it became evident that her sacrifice was to be real and total, not merely a figure of speech. The operation of 1950 was reported in the official press as nothing more than an appendectomy. Nevertheless, it was interpreted in terms of Eva's exhausting schedule and said to have been made more difficult and urgent by virtue of the amount of selfless labour she had taken upon herself for the sake of her people.

Both the armed forces and Eva's illness undoubtedly played an important role in preventing the nomination of Eva Perón for the vice-presidency. The bid made by Eva and those backing her for the office of vice-president of the nation opened a drama that offered both the First Lady and the media a new and powerful statement of the themes of her sacrifice which they had already been making. This occurred in the context of a giant public assembly, the Cabildo Abierto or Open Town Meeting, called to propose the formula Perón-Perón for the coming elections. The secretary general of the CGT at the time, José Espejo, related that during the organization of the event, 'when candidacy was first mentioned to her she eluded a concrete response. But she was in agreement that we should organize a great assembly, because she wanted a popular pronouncement which would support the nomination'.[48]

When the Cabildo Abierto opened its massive session[49] in the late afternoon of August 22, 1950, Perón occupied the place of honour, but his wife was not present. This caused such an uproar among the public that the protests forced the first speaker, José Espejo, to interrupt his speech. He tried to explain that it was undoubtedly Eva's modesty that had made her think she should not make an appearance. But he continued by agreeing that it was obvious that her presence was essential in order to carry on the assembly. Eva appeared within minutes, unable at first to stop weeping in order to speak.

When she was able to manage words, they did not contain an answer to the demands of the assembly that she should accept the candidacy. Near the end of her short speech, she stated 'I will always do what the people may say'. Her audience wildly applauded this, apparently assuming that she had confirmed her acceptance.

However, she went on to repeat a theme common in her oratory from the beginning of her career: 'But I tell you, just as I have said for five years, that I prefer to be Evita rather than the President's wife if "Evita" is said in order to alleviate any pain of my country. Now I say that I continue to prefer to be Evita'. This left her decision unclear, but she concluded without making a more definite declaration.

In her last sentences, startling in retrospect, she actually proclaimed her husband president: 'My general, I, whom the descamisados have declared their plenipotentiary, proclaim you, before the people vote on November 11, President of all Argentinians. The nation is saved because it is governed by General Perón'.

During her husband's speech, which followed Eva's inconclusive statements, someone shouted from the audience, interrupting Perón himself, 'Let the Compañera Eva speak'! The insistence became stronger when the applause for Perón's speech ended. In the face of the clamour for words from Evita, José Espejo directed himself to her, saying, 'Señora, the people are requesting that you accept the position . . .' When she persisted in refusing to speak, he continued, 'Señora, you are the only one who can and must occupy this place'.

At this point, Eva accepted the microphone in order to plead for at least four days in order to reconsider. This was answered by shouts of 'No! No!' and 'Strike!' in the crowd, while heated discussions took place in the official stand. Eva began, 'Compañeros. Compañeros . . ., compañeros. Compañeros: I do not renounce my place in battle, I renounce the honours'. As the audience continued to shout, Eva began to weep again. She was able to say, 'I will do, in the end, what the people decide'. Then, 'Do you believe that, if the post of vice-president were a responsibility and I had been a solution, I would not already have answered yes?'

In the stand different exclamations broke out. Among them, almost disguised by the tumult, was the voice of Perón: 'Stop this act'!

The crowd continued to shout, demanding a decision, while Eva, in growing desperation, begged that she be given time, and that her impatient followers disband. Further confusion in the official stand echoed the popular uproar, while Perón argued with CGT leaders. Finally Espejo announced, 'Compañeros: Compañeros, Evita has requested a two-hour wait. We will stay here. We shall not move until she gives us a favourable reply'. Eva protested, 'This has taken me by surprise . . . Never in my humble Argentinian woman's heart did I think that I could accept this position . . . Give me time to announce my decision to the entire nation by radio'.

The mass of excited people at last dispersed. The press recorded that the position had been accepted, and on August 28, six days later, Eva's candidacy was officially proclaimed by the national secretariat of the CGT. [50] Reports without specific sources state that, at the news of the Perón-Perón formula, military pressures increased with protests not only from Campo de Mayo but from provincial bases as well. [51]

Although Peronists remember August 22, which was actually the date of the Cabildo Abierto, as the Day of Renunciation, Eva Perón did not officially renounce the vice-presidential candidacy until August 31. At eight o'clock that night she read the announcement, stating:

> I realized that I must not change my battle position in the Peronist movement for any other place. . . . This decision comes from the most intimate part of my conscience and for that reason is totally free and has all the force of my definitive will.

Later came the famous statement,

> I do not have in these moments more than one ambition, a single and great personal ambition: that of me it shall be said . . . that there was at the side of Perón a woman who dedicated herself to carrying the hopes of the people to the President, and that the people affectionately called this woman 'Evita'. That is what I want to be.

As reason for her decision Eva declared that

> On October 17 I formulated my permanent vow, before my own conscience: to place myself entirely at the service of the descamisados, who are the humble and the workers. I had an almost infinite debt to pay to them [reference to the part played by the descamisados in demanding the release of Perón in 1945]. I believe I have done all that was in my power to fulfill that vow and to pay my debt.

This explanation has not satisfied many observers. Speculation about the possible real nature of her motives has ranged from the various interpretations of military pressure already mentioned to explanations in terms of her advanced illness. José Espejo [52] himself, who had been one of those to present the project to Eva and one of the most surprised by her final negative, declared that 'She could not be a candidate because she did not believe it correct to compose a presidential formula with a married couple, and she alleged that she should give place to the political sector of the Movement, in the person of Quijano'.

Only three weeks later Eva's deteriorated condition confined her to her room in the presidential residence, where she underwent the last phases of futile medical treatment.

Despite her growing weakness and pain, she defiantly maintained an extraordinary level of activity. The people surrounding her were silent concerning the events of Menéndez's frustrated uprising until all danger had passed. But upon learning of the events of the day Eva insisted on addressing the Peronists over the radio the same evening. The following day, from her sickbed, she negotiated the purchase of arms.

While the news media informed Argentina that Eva was suffering from anaemia and undergoing blood transfusions, her cancer progressed. A flurry of events kept the real nature of her disease from her followers. The first edition of her autobiography *La razón de mi vida* appeared amidst excitement and elaborate ceremony. Just two days later, Eva herself was able to appear at the traditional celebration of October 17, leaving her bed for the first time in more than three weeks. Her weakness was such that her husband was forced to hold her by the waist when she stood. Peronism dedicated this 'Loyalty Day', as the date had been designated, to Eva, while the CGT and Perón himself bestowed decorations on her. At the end of the act, the following day was declared 'Santa Evita's Day' instead of 'San Perón's Day', which had become customary during the years of Peronist government.[53]

In the following weeks Eva Perón apparently underwent two operations. The North American cancer expert, George Pack, whose intervention was secret, performed the first. The second took place in the President Perón Policlinic in Avellaneda under the direction of Ricardo Finochietto, world-famous Argentinian surgeon. Before the latter operation, on November 5, Eva managed to record a speech to be broadcast on November 9. Two days later, on November 11, while she remained prostrate in the hospital, a special ballot box was brought to her bedside so that she could cast her vote in the first Argentinian elections in which the women of the nation participated.[54]

In early December, while the number of masses offered for her health reached the hundreds, Eva managed to recover her strength to the extent that she was able to accompany Perón on short drives around Buenos Aires She later delivered her Christmas speech, and on Christmas Day met with the nation's journalists. The news media still kept the truth of her condition from her public. Her own stubborn resistance in the face of the disease made this task easier. In the context of her continued audiences with union delegations, the statement in the press in mid-March that she would soon renew her activity in Labour and Welfare did not seem to be the absurdity that it actually was.[55] Only a few days later the Agrarian Plan Eva Perón was launched by the Foundation, making mechanical equipment accessible to farmers in order to increase the nation's acreage under cultivation.[56]

Her last public appearances encouraged still more exaggerated hope of her recovery. But only a nearly superhuman dedication and determination could have made them possible. She not only appeared at the assembly in celebration of Labour Day, but she managed to give a short speech, the last and one of the most violent of her career. A week later, on her birthday, she appeared briefly on a terrace of the presidential residence to greet the crowds which had gathered. She was unable to stand alone. That day, at the suggestion of Héctor J. Cámpora, then president of the Chamber of Deputies, Congress designated Evita the 'Spiritual Chief of the Nation'. On May 23, she addressed the governors and provincial legislators in the residence, again with a definite element of violence in her rhetoric.

She made her final public appearance at the inauguration of Perón's second term in office, June 5, 1952. In order to stand, she had to resort to the use of a specially constructed support of wire and plaster. With this aid she stood by her husband's side in the open car in which they drove in triumph from the presidential residence to the Congressional Palace and then to the Pink House. She endured the rest of the ceremony standing.[57]

Even confined to her bed Eva attempted to be active, writing a book, *Mi mensaje* ('My Message'), never completed. Outside, the life of the nation seemed slowly to shift its centre to revolve around the dying First Lady. The newspapers included periodical reports on her health. Groups continually passed the presidential residence asking about her state, or stationed themselves for a time in vigil. Congress occupied itself for days in early July with a project of converting the monument to the descamisado, which Evita had proposed in 1951, into a memorial structure in which Eva herself would be buried.[58] It was to be the largest monument in the world. At the same time the news reached Buenos Aires that North American publishers had refused to issue an edition of *La razón de mi vida*. In repudiation of this attitude in particular and imperialism in general, a strike was called on July 4, eliciting praises for the author and expressions of solidarity with the project of her monument. On July 17, the book was declared an obligatory text for the national schools. The following day Eva received the Necklace of the Order of the Liberator San Martín, made of platinum and gold and resplendent with precious stones.[59]

During this period, the prayers and masses for Eva's recovery continued throughout Argentina, culminating in a mass for her recovery organized by the CGT in the centre of the widest avenue of Buenos Aires. Eva's confessor, Hernán Benítez, addressed the people gathered for the service as well as the rest of the nation to which his words were broadcast. His speech declared Eva the martyr of the descamisados, an example given by God to the Argentinian people of self-sacrifice and faith.[60] Meanwhile, the prayers of the popular classes of neighbouring countries were offered for the salvation of the Argentinian First Lady.[61]

Eva Perón had already been dead for two minutes when the radio announcement of the Subsecretariat of Information of the Presidency fixed the hour of her death at the more easily remembered time of 8:25, the evening of July 26, 1952. Within two hours Dr. Pedro Ara, noted Spanish embalmer, began the preparations of the corpse necessary before its exhibition the following day.[62] Perón had made arrangements to bury the deceased First Lady in the Convent of San Francisco. But later the same night, after some vacillation, he granted the petition of the CGT to have the body of Eva placed in its headquarters until the mausoleum in her monument should be ready for her.

With the procession that accompanied the body to its funeral chapel in the Ministry of Labour and Welfare, Eva's posthumous odyssey began. It perhaps ended only in 1975, after twenty-three years, first of public display, later of secret transport, plots and burials and finally exhumation and return to Argentina.

A monumental procession carried her to the first of many places of temporary rest. It also marked the first phase of a grandiose funeral and subsequent massive mourning, which was to be the focus of some of the bitterest criticism produced by the opposition. The pomp and the extreme forms of public mourning which the regime imposed officially and which much of popular Peronism assumed spontaneously were not, however, unique in Argentinian history. The burial of another First Lady, Encarnación Ezcurra de Rosas, slightly more than a century earlier, parallels the homage paid to Eva Perón on a startling number of points. Since the original *coup d'état* of which Perón had formed part, official funerals like that of Vice President Quijano in April 1952, had been given an emotional tone. One great difference between the treatment of official publicity of Eva's and Quijano's deaths is immediately obvious, however: the death and funeral of Quijano occupied the official press for only two days, after which no mention is made of them.[63]

A continually passing mass of mourners kept the vigil by the body of their Evita, entering in double file and leaving through another door without stopping by the coffin. Outside the edifice of Labour and Welfare the famous waiting queues of Argentinians who had come to gaze at the dead leader for the last time stretched up to 35 blocks. Walls of flowers channelled the mourners toward the building where the body lay.

As the days passed, the numbers became so great and the wait so long that the services of Public Health, the Foundation Eva Perón, and the Army took on the responsibility of providing hygienic facilities, blankets and stretchers, and hot drinks with food. At the sight of the silent files, Juan Perón turned to Raúl Apold and remarked, 'I never knew they loved her so much. I never knew they loved her so'.[64]

Perón at first announced that 'the wake shall continue a month, or, if necessary, two, until the last citizen of the Republic has been able to see Compañera Evita'. However, the demands of the preservation treatment carried out by Dr. Ara cut this short. On August 1, the public learned that the funeral chapel would remain open only ten more days, due to the process of conservation 'which will give her absolute corporeal permanence, complying thus—in this also—with the will expressed by the illustrious invalid'.[65]

On August 9 another procession carried the coffin to the National Congress, and the lines of mourners followed. Two days later, a gun-carriage bore the body from Congress to the Central Obrera. Nine police patrol cars preceded the coffin, while thirty-five men and ten women dressed in white shirts—symbol of the descamisados—and black skirts or trousers pulled the carriage. On either side marched cadets of the military academies in formation with students from the

Student City (*Ciudad Estudiantil*) of Eva's creation as well as nurses from the Foundation Eva Perón. Along the route followed by the procession, 17,000 soldiers kept back a throng of 2,000,000 waiting to watch the Lady of Hope pass by.[66]

Ara's work began, and the watch kept by Eva's people over her body ended. But their vigil continued at the side of the small altars that had begun to be constructed alongside the waiting queues of mourners as well as all over the country. Funeral ceremonies had been held in cemeteries throughout Argentina. In Chivilcoy her portrait was said to have been deposited in the mausoleum of the Duartes —the family who had rejected her as a child.[67]

Eva's martyrdom was complete. The theme was reiterated in official accounts and ceremonies and in public homages. Her image as a martyr lacked only official recognition. As early as July 31 only five days after her death, the Sindicato de Obreros y Empleados de la Industria de la Alimentación telegraphed Pope Pius requesting that he confer upon her his blessing and sainthood. In November the Agrupación de Trabajadores Latinamericanos Sindicalizados repeated the request, proposing that Eva be made the saint of all American workers.[68]

Once again, as in the time of her illness, official publicity sought to fill the vacuum left in the many places she had occupied during her years of health and power. Even her corporeal presence in the form of an embalmed body seems to have played a part in this campaign. The prolonged funerary rites, themselves made possible by the embalming process, established a palpable contact with the deceased Evita. Official reports emphasized that postal boxes still existed in which letters to Eva could be placed, continuing the illusion of a link with the dead woman. Although the correspondence actually went to the Foundation, the poor of Argentina could still perform an act that had been important to them for years: they were still able to 'write to Evita'.[69] School children read from *La razón de mi vida* daily as well as from texts with pages dedicated to Eva's work in life, to her continued existence, often as a star, and to unceasing vigilance over her descamisados after death.

The annual celebration of occasions such as her birth, her renouncement of the vice-presidency, and her death also kept Evita before the public. Peronism dedicated the first October 17 after her death, like the last during her life, to Eva as Spiritual Chief of the Nation. Even the very moment of her death was constantly recalled as the nightly news broadcasts began, 'It is 8.25, the hour in which Eva Perón passed into immortality'.

These invocations of the presence of Eva meant that her image still functioned as intermediary between Perón and his people, between governmental machinery and governed masses. Months after her death, when her final testament was read to her waiting followers, her words continued to affirm that 'I will feel myself forever close to the people, and I will continue to be the bridge of love stretched between the descamisados and Perón'.[70]

Simultaneously, Perón began attempts to serve as the bridge between his dead wife and popular Peronism.[71] This, however, succeeded only as publicity: Perón left Eva's personal tasks to others soon after he had taken them on amid tremendous journalistic fanfare.

During the three years that remained before the end of the Peronist régime, the homage paid to Eva reached flamboyant extremes in official circles. For her monument, collections were made, earth from different provinces and countries donated, and electricity, major drainage pipes, and traffic detoured. Despite these practical and financial preparations, the structure still consisted of nothing more than a foundation at the time of the fall of Perón.[72]

With the end of the Peronist government, the rejoicing anti-Peronists denounced Eva and all associated with her. The crowds destroyed her statues and busts and burned everything bearing her name, from books to blankets. Early in its brief period in power, the government of General Lonardi organized an exhibit to which the public was invited to see the clothes and jewels of Eva Perón, displayed in glass cases, each carefully labelled with its price.[73]

Special commissions[74] arranged for the sale of the possessions of Eva Perón, especially her jewels, for incorporation into the 'state patrimony'. The government deposited the funds resulting from the auction in an account especially created for that purpose. The riches represented by this account were always exaggerated in the minds of Eva's enemies, where they were augmented by speculation on the amount of funds in the Swiss bank accounts of the wife of the deposed President. The correct figures concerning these funds were apparently a secret of ex-President Pedro Aramburu, confided to at least one friend who in turn divulged the cipher only after the assassination of Aramburu in 1970. Sources with access to these figures placed the amount deposited in Switzerland in the name of María Eva Duarte de Perón at $700,000,000—calculated to be the equivalent of the funds of the Rockefeller Foundation.[75]

The purpose to which the fortune obtained from the sale of the jewels was dedicated is still undetermined. Eva's acrimoniously disputed wealth apparently remains in Switzerland. The funds, it is said, can be withdrawn only with special documentation, which must be provided by the Argentinian government. The money had thus supposedly become an object of negotiation between the non-Peronist governments and Juan Domingo Perón. Since Eva's name was never legally María Eva Duarte nor, therefore, María Eva Duarte de Perón, only the Argentinian authorities can produce documents proving that the owner of Eva's account was actually the woman who was the wife of Juan Perón.[76]

If Lonardi's purpose in exhibiting Eva's treasures and denouncing her private fortune was to discredit her in the eyes of her followers, he failed, as have all who have used this as an argument against the Peróns since their time in power. In the eyes of the Argentinians who had faith in the word of their leader, her wealth was justified by the purposes for which she had accumulated it, as revealed in the final testament[77] read to her followers in the Plaza de Mayo after her death:

> While Perón may live, he may do what he wishes with all my possessions . . . but after Perón, the only inheritor of my possessions must be the people, to demand, by whatever means, the inexorable fulfilment of this wish . . .
>
> I would like a permanent fund of social aid to be created with these possessions for cases of collective misfortunes which affect the poor, and I hope that they accept this as one more proof of my affection. I would hope, for example, that in these cases a subsidy be granted for each family of at least the wages and salaries of one year.
>
> Also I desire that, with this permanent fund of Evita, scholarships be instituted so that the children of the workers might study and be, thus, defenders of the doctrine of Perón . . .
>
> My jewels do not belong to me. The greater part were gifts from my people. I do not want them ever to fall into the hands of the oligarchy, and therefore, I will that they constitute, in the museum of Peronism, a permanent value which may only be used in direct benefit of the people.
>
> May my jewels thus, as gold backs the money of some countries, back

a permanent credit which will open the banks of the country in benefit of the people, to the end that housing may be constructed for the workers of my country.

When Lonardi came to power, his government formed a commission to authenticate the corpse as that of Eva and to determine whether or not to remove it from its resting place in the syndicate headquarters. When the commission could produce no technical reason for its removal, officialdom left the enbalmed body as it was. At the same time, the Peronists formed a 'Commission for the Recuperation of the Remains of Eva Perón', headed by Elsa Chamorro, who was named personal representative of Perón. Meanwhile, the Duarte family petitioned the government for the possession of the corpse.[78]

When, two months after the 'Liberating Revolution', Lonardi was in turn deposed, rumours of attempted kidnappings of the body by either Peronists or anti-Peronists became more insistent. Finally, late in December, Lieutenant Colonel Carlos Eugenio Moore Koening, chief of the Intelligence Service of the army, who was in charge of the safe-keeping of the corpse, decided to remove the remains in order to give them a Christian burial, as he himself defined his purpose. Moore Koening, declaring that his initiative was authorized by Aramburu, arrived with three other military men at the CGT headquarters during the night, when the guard consisted only of ten midshipmen under the command of four naval officers. Eva's embalmer was also present, observing the condition of his work. His protests produced a receipt for the rosary and the bejewelled coat of arms which were removed with the body. The corpse was placed in a coffin bought for that purpose and, with the help of four workers who happened to be in the building, taken to a waiting truck.[79]

After two weeks of removal from one place to another, the embalmed body was placed in the building of the Information Service of the State, where it was hidden in a box labelled 'radio equipment'. At this point, Moore Koening apparently travelled to Chile under orders from President Aramburu, in order to offer Juana Ibarguren, Eva's mother, the remains of her daughter. In this way Aramburu and Moore Koening hoped to prevent the legal representative of Perón from obtaining the corpse. Although the mother of the deceased continued her negotiations with the Argentinian government, and different governments over the years continued their promises to her, nothing ever came of her hopes to bury her daughter with her family.[80]

Whatever the reason, the corpse remained among other crates containing broadcasting materials until June 8, 1956. Moore Koening's successor as director of the Information Service, Colonel Mario Cabanillas, accidentally discovered the body while reviewing the contents of the boxes in the edifice. When the President of the nation was informed of the incident, the order for Christian burial was reissued and the head of the Casa Militar, Captain Francisco Manrique, was placed in charge of the operation.[81]

Later versions, based on documents of the Army Information Service (Servicio de Informaciones del Ejército: SIE) permit further reconstruction of events. Apparently the SIE issued an order for the remains to be put in the hands of a Jesuit priest, now dead, identified by the initials C.D.T. On January 4, 1957, this priest delivered to President Aramburu documents that testified that he had disposed of the corpse and ensured the secrecy of its resting place by sending off five identical coffins to different destinations. In the presence of Manrique, Aramburu appended a note, stating:

> The Commander-in-Chief of the Armed Forces, one year after my death, shall proceed to return the remains to the nearest relative if by doing so national peace and understanding are promoted.

The papers were placed in a sealed envelope and deposited with a notary. One year after Aramburu's kidnapping and murder in 1970, the notary presented the envelope to President Lanusse, who was also Commander-in-Chief of the Armed Forces.[82]

Envoys of the Argentinian government disentombed the body in Milan, Italy. Lanusse returned the corpse to Juan Perón at his residence in exile in Madrid, claiming that he did so as a goodwill gesture in the process of building national unity. The move formed part of his attempt to open dialogue with Peronists in Argentina and negotiations with Perón in Spain. For two years the corpse remained in Madrid, in the mansion occupied by Perón and his third wife, Isabel Martínez. Peronists in Argentina demanded its return to Eva's homeland. Others claimed that the body was exhumed in order to cause Perón's death by heart attack: the deceased was decapitated, they said; her legs broken, and her breasts torn open. The reappearance of the corpse may have engendered as much or more dissatisfaction and bitterness as rejoicing.

In late 1972, Juan and Isabel Perón were called to Buenos Aires to head a new Peronist régime. Only a year and a half later, Perón was dead, and Isabel, carefully emulating Eva's dress, coiffure and gestures, had become President of the nation. During this period, although Eva appeared constantly in official publicity, her corpse remained in Madrid.

Finally, in November, 1974, in the midst of rumours of a split between the government and labour, Isabel moved to bring the body of her predecessor back to Buenos Aires in an attempt to marshal popular support for the government. Mounting a heavy guard at the site of the arrival, the régime televised the return of Eva Perón to her people. The jet with its precious cargo taxied to a halt, and while onlookers stood at attention, double doors slid open, revealing the coffin of the enbalmed body. Contrary to expectations of a wave of popular reaction to the event, Eva's subsequent move to the side of Perón, also embalmed and preserved in the Presidential residence, caused little commotion. Almost a year later, the body was moved yet again, to be buried for a second time. The odyssey may have ended. But, Argentinians ask, where is she really? Has Evita returned to a cemetery in Junín? Is she in a specially armoured vault in Buenos Aires' most aristocratic cemetery, La Recoleta? Any grave marked with her name may be empty. And the corpse that suddenly re-appeared and seemed from a distance to be Eva Perón—that corpse, some Argentinians whisper, may have been a wax doll all along.

4

The Myths

The Lady of Hope and the Woman of the Black Myth

THE LADY OF HOPE

On the pampas a delicately beautiful blonde child struggled to overcome the obstacles of humble birth, poverty, and isolation. Eva Duarte had been born in 1919, the year of the massacres of the Semana Trágica, which had demonstrated the most brutal form reactions to labour unrest could assume. At seven, she had seen powerful relatives of her father refuse her mother, siblings, and herself entry to his wake and funeral: Eva's family was despised as the deceased's concubine and illegitimate offspring. If this father and lover had done nothing to dispel their financial difficulties and notoriety, society would do nothing to mitigate them. Yet, despite these obstacles constantly before her, the family's youngest, Evita, trustingly applied herself to the development of a talent for drama. This, she dreamed, would take her away to a very different life as an actress in the great city of Buenos Aires.

As a young teenager she managed to convince others of her gift. A well-known tango singer and his troupe passed through her town on tour, and the star himself agreed to allow her to travel with them to Buenos Aires. In the capital, the fifteen-year-old stepped off the train into the glass and steel of the Retiro terminals only to find human conditions in the city little improved over the injustices of country life. Her few contacts proved to be of little use. Evita Duarte began from the very bottom, her own tenacity and industry only gradually overcoming the tremendous odds set against her, a little provincial alone in an unknown world.

Finally successful, and for the first time prosperous, Eva established herself as a rising star of Argentinian radio. To crown her success, one version of the tale recounts, she purchased an apartment in the most elegant and aristocratic neighbourhood of Buenos Aires, Barrio Norte. [1]

She had by then reached her mature beauty, but was still so slender that her loveliness would always be childlike. And Evita was learning to accentuate the fine lines of her face and body with the classically simple clothes and hairstyle which would later render her image timeless.

As she advanced her career, the conditions in which she worked and observed others working with her could only sharpen the innate social conscience she had brought with her from her childhood in the Argentinian interior. In the course of her activities in labour and charitable concerns, Eva attended a benefit given for the victims of the catastrophic earthquake in the province of San Juan. There she met Colonel Juan Domingo Perón.

Their love at first sight revealed Perón to her as the source of her future identity. She immediately began to work for him and with him, forming herself into an extension of his ideas and personality. Perón found room for the young actress in his Secretariat of Labour and Welfare, where she for the first time tried her hand at what was to be her life's work.

When the opposition toppled Colonel Perón from his pinnacle of rapidly consolidating power, Eva Duarte was suddenly alone in a city that associated her with the banished man. Risking her life, she went out into the streets to attempt the impossible: engineering Perón's return to his people and to her. Her efforts among the powerful soon proved fruitless. Undiscouraged, she turned to the working class, persuading its leaders, appealing to the workers themselves, organizing meetings, and promulgating the cause of her man and her people. Finally, on October 17, she watched the march from the factories to the House of Government and heard the crowds demand the return of Perón.

Soon Evita Duarte was Señora María Eva Duarte de Perón, a figure attracting increasing attention in her position as the wife of Perón. Her followers initially saw her popularity as deriving from the fascination which Perón himself exercised over the *descamisados*; later they continued to insist that her magic was his. She, the ideal wife, merged her being with her husband's. She immersed herself in his interests, concerned herself with his worries, and shouldered his cause. Her energies and ideas submitted to the direction of his. Although she appeared to exercise initiative, she, as a woman in love with a man, in fact did not: projects or ideas that seemed to have originated as her responsibility actually owed their existence to the man she loved, or to circumstance.[2]

In this relationship, Eva created a perfect matrimony. Not only did she remain constantly and irreproachably faithful to Perón, but she carefully muted the sexual element in her marriage. She affirmed, through the books attributed to her authorship, that she and her husband expressed their love for each other through their concern and love for the *descamisados* of Argentina. The letters the imprisoned Perón wrote her from exile did not declare his love for her, but instead asked only that she take care of 'his "workers" '. This, Eva realized, was his most deeply felt word of love, and she learned to respond in the same terms: 'Since that time, when I for my part want to express to him my love as a woman . . . I also find no *purer* nor greater way than to offer him a little of my life, burning it out for the love of his "descamisados" '.[3] 'You know how much I love Perón,' she pronounced in a speech, 'but for a long time I have not considered myself the wife of Perón. I consider myself an Argentine woman and an idealist, who . . . confronting the responsibility of the fatherland, forgets everything.'[4] When Perón wished to reward her, she wrote in *La Razón de mi Vida*, he gave his wife a kiss, which he placed, she was careful to say, 'on the forehead'.[5]

Eva's unrelenting efforts for her people contributed to the special form her relationship with her husband assumed. Their dedication led them both to keep impossibly long hours. But Eva, an incorrigible Bohemian, could not change her habits of working late at night, nor could Perón, equally unchangeable as a military man, change his compulsion of beginning his endless days as early as possible. Eva would return from her office just as Perón was preparing to leave for his. Later, the Lady of Hope's labour of love marked her more definitively still, exacerbating her illness and finally making sexual relations impossible for her for years before she finally died.

Eva unquestioningly followed her emotions as she sought out

roles to fill as First Lady of her country. 'In us [women],' the Eva Perón of *La Razon de mi Vida* continues to tell her readers, 'the intellect develops in the shadow of the heart, and therefore the intellect only sees through the lenses of love.'[6] Eva worked on the basis of the intuition that flowed, not from the intellect, but from the heart. Never taking the initiative, never assertive, never using force, at a peak of activity this Evita radiated love and peace.

Claiming that she knew nothing about politics, she found in social work a sphere for which her womanly intuition and emotional life qualified her perfectly. She dedicated much of this work to children, as would be expected from such an ideally feminine, thus deeply maternal, woman. A woman may involve herself in any area of activity to which her man directs her, but her place and the function for which she was born are in the home. Neither Eva's childlessness nor her death affects this theme in any way. Eva Perón had no sons and daughters of her own; she was mother to the children of Argentina. More than that, she was mother of the nation as a whole, particularly to the common people and the poor and needy of Argentina. It was maternal devotion that motivated her attendance on the poor, her work to raise money for her cause, her conferences with governors of the provinces, and her meetings with labour delegations. In grateful response, popular Peronism dubbed her its Lady of Hope and Good Fairy.

Not even the invitation of the Spanish government to visit her nation's Motherland could make Eva forget the workers and their cause. She continued to stress her interest in social work and to distribute alms throughout her journey. But the deeds of the Good Fairy of the poor now had to share the spotlight with the successful social contacts of the travelling First Lady. The Spaniards welcomed her with protocol usually reserved for royalty. Soon she had become as much a favourite with the Spanish aristocrats as with the hundreds of thousands of anonymous Spaniards who lined the streets to catch sight of her. In Italy too she fascinated both the crowds and high society. Only her decision to change her itinerary prevented her arrival in London from being, as sumptuous preparations for it promised, one of the most important events of high society's year. The innumerable rooms of a mansion in the heart of the London frequented by English aristocracy awaited her in vain.

Europe, even France, the supreme authority on matters of feminine taste, marvelled at the beauty of Argentina's emissary of good will. She encountered admiration everywhere, confirming her position as a paragon of elegance. Her followers memorized the details of her every change of dress—the fittings, the designers, the gold lamé, the hats, mantillas, even a tiara—and never tired of the rainbow of images that spread over the media of the time and continued glowing in the huge full-coloured photographs of magazines still dedicated, twenty-five years later, exclusively to her.

But Eva did not spend all her time dispensing charity, making calls, and planning her wardrobe. She made a point of visiting museums and attending cultural events, appreciating deeply these works and performances, which she went out of her way to see. As always properly hesitant to express inexpert opinions on politics, Eva Perón expatiated on her preferences in music and literature.

From her triumphal tour of Europe, the First Lady returned to throw herself immediately into her campaign for women's suffrage in Argentina. A week after her arrival in Buenos Aires, she directed an open letter to Argentinian women from the front pages of the newspapers, announcing her plans and the needs for their fulfillment. Eva explicitly differentiated her movement from feminist movements in other, especially Anglo-Saxon, countries, where the Peronists felt that feminism had become a form of competition with men. Eva and Peronism rejected earlier Argentinian campaigns on behalf of women's civil rights as copies of foreign ideas, considering them not only mistaken in content, but the result of ingrained social snobbery and cultural imperialism.

The virtue of the Peronist woman lay in never aspiring to supplant the opposite sex. Rather, Peronist feminism represented an effort to take advantage of women's own special identity and talents in order better to fill their particular place in the world. Peronist women carefully emphasized the point that they had no intention of denying their domestic nature now that they had obtained full citizenship.

Eva Perón's position in the nation exemplified the position of the ideal woman in the home. She, on her level, like the housewife on hers, assumed a role as the chief agent responsible for the transmission of the values which uphold society as a whole. Both carried out functions broader than spiritually and physically nutritive ones. The watchfulness of the Peronist woman over domestic economy and morality extended beyond the home to become one of her special political functions: it was she who, qualified by her feminine nature, could best take up a unique watch against treachery within the Peronist movement and threats arising from without. Evita, chief protector of the movement, kept watch as well over its leader and her husband, Juan Perón himself. He, realizing her importance as his shield against betrayal and evil acknowledged that 'Eva . . . with her marvellous judgement has been the guardian of my life, confided to her intelligence and loyalty.' [7]

With her successes in Europe and in the campaign for women's rights behind her, Eva's activities grew in importance and number. Her influence depended on her all-enveloping aura more than on specific actions affecting particular political situations, despite the fact that the Peronist press of the time offered reports on her activities of particulars of personages, organizations, schedules, gifts, and honours. Eva defined the tone of Peronism as a movement even more than as a party.

As she wore herself out in her office day by day, the symptoms of her final disease began to appear, bearing witness to the gruelling sacrifice that Eva insisted on offering up for her people. 'Poor thing,' stated a Peronist referring to the widely known fact that sexual relations were impossible for Eva for two years before her death, 'She gave up even her happiness as a woman for us.' [8] In her attempts to continue working through her long illness, the Lady of Hope was making her conscious and voluntary sacrifice.

Her renunciation of the vice-presidency formed part of this process. In the mass demonstration of the Cabildo Abierto, the Open Town Hall, Eva's people and her party offered her the highest honour which they could bestow. When she refused this honour, her ·disappointed followers dedicated the nearby anniversary of October 17 to her in recognition of her selfless renunciation. The words 'Santa Evita' appeared for the first time in the press in connection with this celebration. [9]

Her death, which loomed before her immediately after the Renunciation, made her martyrdom incontrovertible. Her brokenhearted followers responded to the dead Eva in the only way appropriate to her saintly act: they worshipped her as a saint. They erected altars to her; offered her prayers; called her their Spiritual Chief, Saint Eva, and Spiritual Protector of the Argentine University; believed in her miraculous powers and waited for her return.

THE WOMAN OF THE BLACK MYTH

I. Eva the Bad

'That woman', '*esa mujer*', was born in the ill-disguised brothel of her mother. During a childhood and adolescence spent helping to run and maintain her family's 'boarding house' or 'pension', Eva early began to attract the attention of passing clients as well as the towns-people in general. Already aggressive and ambitious at fifteen, she linked herself to the troupe of a tango singer whom she had probably seduced, and travelled to Buenos Aires to establish herself as a prostitute. Her professed occupation on the stage was no more than a disguise of her real activities.

The capital offered Eva a whirlwind of affairs with actors, pro-ducers, industrialists, and political figures. She possessed a coarse, dark attraction, a typically provincial prettiness. But beyond this, she demonstrated sexual appetites and habits that contributed spectacularly to her notoriety. Exploiting both her liaisons and the special talents that attracted them, Eva was frantically scrambling up the social ladder when she met Juan Domingo Perón and im-mediately moved in with him. Recognizing his rising star, she held on to this catch—with success which amazed even her: anti-Peronists say that when Perón proposed marriage, Evita Duarte was so astounded that she nearly fell out of bed.

Sometimes the account differs. Eva could magnetize Perón be-cause she, like him, lacked sexuality. Either she was frigid and he, impotent, or both valued power over all. Even sexual attraction became unimportant beside this all-consuming passion. Their dis-torted values led them to centre their lives entirely around the in-terests of their régime, to the extent that they did not sleep together—Perón, the military man, rising early, and Eva, the bohemian, retir-ing as he rose.

However she attracted him, Eva Duarte married Juan Perón and immediately began to wear the pants in their relationship. Unlike women such as Eleanore Roosevelt of the United States or Madame Auriol of France who know how to play 'the role of second violin which every woman of real tact assumes',[10] Eva took up the first violin or even the baton of the orchestra. She contrasted dramatically with the ideal wife who 'has neither youth, nor fur coats, nor [knows] how to harangue over the radio, but knows how to knit, cooks well, darns the socks and bakes pastries which make you lick your fingers'.[11] This perfect wife satisfies any man simply by being 'a woman who is quiet, intuitive, and who does not make speeches'.[12]

The dominance of this upstart soon extended beyond her marriage. She involved herself in all aspects of government. Perón meekly endorsed her growing interference by asserting that wherever Eva appeared, she represented his own presence and carried his authority. The sun of a radiant Eva began to eclipse Juan's fading moon. Eva was converting the nation into a matriarchy.

Inexorably, she stretched her web of control over the other men in her husband's régime. Some she dominated through the fascination of her own eroticism or through secret sexual practices. Others Eva Perón castrated—sometimes figuratively and sometimes literally: she dealt with her own underlings by rendering them political eunuchs, and she tortured her opponents with electric shocks that left them impotent. Eva took direct responsibility for the castration of rebel leaders and others, making flamboyant display of her satisfaction with her deed. She kept a glass receptacle preserving the testicles of her victims in the office where she leaned, young and exquisitely clad in her Parisian suits, over a desk to attend the needs recited by ministers, union delegations, and the poor alike.

Meanwhile, the new First Lady attempted in vain to shoulder her way into social circles closed to her. When her efforts failed, she determined to outdo the aristocratic women who would not accept her. Her envy of these inaccessible social circles had decided her marriage to Perón, a rising young military figure. Now that she was First Lady, her bitter resentfulness intensified. It sent her to Europe; drove her to establish the vast Eva Perón Foundation; goaded her into the acquisition of houses, jewels, and clothes; and, finally, kindled her frustrated appeal to the masses for the recognition denied her by high society.

Early in her husband's régime, she had attended an exclusive fashion show in Harrod's department store, only to be ignored or, according to some accounts, to be left alone with her small party of friends as the distinguished ladies swept out. The same women refused her the traditional honour bestowed upon Presidents' wives, the office of president of their charity organization, the Sociedad de Beneficiencia. Their acts only exacerbated Eva's long-standing resentment towards those whose social position she could never attain. This rancour became unbearable and prodded her into expressing it in every aspect of her life, accounting for most of her projects; she knit even the beneficial works of her charity into her elaborate plots of retaliation.

Her petty desire for vengeance far outweighed any political convictions or motivations Eva might have claimed. An anti-Peronist with a nondescript surname would run no risk from the same activities for which Eva would jail anyone with one of the aristocratic surnames of Buenos Aires. It was Eva Perón who imprisoned upper class women and adolescents accused of demonstrating against the government. Knowing that this would inflict greater cruelty on the sheltered members of the upper classes than on middle-class anti-Peronists, Eva jailed the women with prostitutes and drug addicts. In some cases, the First Lady threatened to interfere with the funerals of older women of the aristocracy, preventing their relatives from burying them with their illustrious forebears. However, if the ladies in question invited her to tea in their homes, she promised that the funeral plans would go through.

Eva's drive to obtain the marks of her enemies' social status found its most complete and extravagant expression in her tour of Europe. However, as would have been expected, the lamentable cultural deprivation inherent in her disreputable origins foiled her prodigious efforts.

On her wardrobe alone, in her attempts to surpass her enemies, she lavished millions of dollars. Before Eva's trip to Europe, an anti-Peronist took the trouble to count her different outfits and reported to the press that during the 270 days between June 4, 1946 and April 30, 1947 the First Lady had donned 306 dresses.[13]

Original models began to arrive by official airplane from Paris. Some of these, bouffant, gala gowns, occupied an entire plane, which the Argentinian government sent to France and brought back at public expense, containing the dress arranged on a solitary standing mannequin.

All of this could not change the Eva who had peered out of one of her first publicity posters, smiling under 'a funny little hat from the movies'.[14] This Evita, shamelessly and gaudily voluptuous, lurked forever behind the later more streamlined image that diet and expensive clothes created. At the time of her European trip she still revealed her own true penchant for a wardrobe that was distinctly Hollywood-esque, her taste expressing itself in elaborate falls and rolls of blonde hair and in an addiction to fur wraps even in the hottest Spanish and Italian weather. Even when her clothes lost the stamp of her early career, she could not hide the tell-tale signs of her vulgar origins: her wide hips and thick ankles.

Her endeavours to convince the world of her appreciation of literature and the arts met with little more success. She was hard put to disguise her interest in art as anything other than what it was: an emotion inspired by the value of a piece in terms of money or status. Her fascination with the Prado in Madrid ended after her questions about the worth of various paintings. When Eva declared that her favourite composer was Chopin and her favourite author Plutarch, anti-Peronists responded with disbelief, certain that these were no more than ornaments in her façade. 'Chopin?' they asked, 'Chopin? ... Can it be some sort of pseudonym for a composer of tangos?'[14] As for Plutarch, they could be sure that anyone unable to speak correct Spanish would scarcely pick up volumes of heavy classical prose for her preferred reading.

Eva's poor language indelibly marked her as what she was, despite any attempts to erase her past. Not only did she use Argentinian idioms considered improper in the First Lady of the nation, but she knew no grammar. Beyond this, she shocked many with her use of rough or obscene expressions. When she used long sophisticated words and phrases, it was obvious to her enemies that she was hiding her lack of education behind complex language which she herself could not understand.

These failures only frustrated her strivings to ascend to the revered heights of the accepted Argentinian social scale. Eva set out to prove that European society would welcome her. Her desire to gain rank for herself sent her to an audience with the Pope, from which she had hoped to emerge a Pontifical Marquise. When she did not, she went on to establish contact with royalty at any cost. Her visit with ex-King Umberto of Italy satisfied only Eva: her enemies scoffed at her choice of a mere former king, which proved that Eva's search for a king, any king, with whom to be seen had aborted. The pointed lack of cordiality from Buckingham Palace confirmed the fact that true royalty would not consider receiving her.

Eva's desire to avenge these bitter disappointments led into increasingly violent paroxysms of fury. She fell into states of pathological emotional disarray when crossed, or when she worked herself into the rages typical of her public speeches. She herself assumed personal responsibility for the régime's secret police and took pleasure in placing herself in charge of torture meted out to Perón's opponents.

At the height of this bloody career, Eva Perón fell ill. Her disease progressed over the months until finally she lay dying, her body emanating mysterious odours of putrefaction. She was rotting while still alive.

Her followers were already in paroxysms of grief when their Evita was suddenly dead. The entire nation of Peronists threw itself into a delirium of mass mourning maintained with sacrifices to the dead Spiritual Leader of the Nation. Altars sprang up everywhere bearing paintings and photographs of the smiling martyr. The bereaved populace offered pagan prayers and rites up to its heroine not only in their homes, where flowers and candles decked the altars, but in public—in the plazas and party centres, and in the queue that stretched block after block through the city where the mourners waited for the chance to bid Evita a last farewell at the side of her coffin. They transformed their wait in 'la cola' into an orgy of distorted forms of worship of the dead leader—uncontrolled and uncontrollable exhibitions of their physiological impulses.

The myth of Eva began to grow, gripping the ignorant masses with unrelenting power. Her people heaped exaggerated praises on her, comparing her in Congress with Joan of Arc, Catherine de Medici, Elizabeth I of England, Isabel the Catholic of Spain, and the Virgin Mary herself. Eva Perón became the Spiritual Chief of the Nation, the Mother of the Poor, and Saint Evita. Peronists revered her as Virgin of the Unsheltered and Madre María, the name of a popular Argentinian faith healer, or *curandera*. Motivated by mystical love, Peronism set out to construct the largest monument in the world in which to lay the embalmed body.

The prayers and rites of the mourners did not disappear as time passed, but began to crystallize around the myth as a cult. The working classes continued to intone 'Saint María Eva who art in Heaven', while some believed that they saw Eva in the sky, her profile clearly imprinted on the moon. During Perón's troubles with the church, Peronist women formed a Congregation of Our Lady Eva Duarte de Perón and donned nuns' robes in honour of their patroness to serve the party. A bust of Eva somewhere in the Argentinian interior began to cause miraculous cures.

Meanwhile the corpse of the embalmed Eva, the central relic, held sway over the cult and its members. Peronists, believing a prophecy that those who possessed the remains would also hold power in government, prepared to do battle to protect the beautiful corpse. When it disappeared after the fall of Perón, its power did not diminish. The danger grew that it could, by its reappearance, arouse the masses to a frenzy that would cause a turning point in Argentinian history. And Eva's followers over the years demanded and waited this reappearance: Peronists and anti-Peronists alike knew that the embalmed woman could be destroyed by fire alone.

Eva the Good

Eva's base past, although it stigmatized her forever, also tempered her. She emerged from the gutter, armed with force, character, and conviction. Such an Eve may have been evil, locked in conflict with another agent of evil, her husband. But she may also have ingenuously allowed an evil Perón to exploit her goodness and strength; or this strength may have been such that it dominated Perón himself.

A good Eva could have submitted to unscrupulous manipulation of her husband, genuinely unaware that differences existed between them and that he was using her for his purposes. The plots of the men around her reduced her to an innocent tool of evil. Perón supported her efforts to champion the poor out of mere opportunism and hypocrisy. Seeing that the young Evita hypnotized the popular masses, he exploited her charm and enthusiasm in order further to exploit the crowds under her spell.

Eva, however, in a struggle with Perón never visible to the public, may have proved herself a force to be reckoned with, and to which he had to submit until her death removed her threat to him. In their earliest days together, while Perón longed only for peace, Eva insisted on a drive for power. When his friends betrayed him and his enemies threatened him with exile, Perón immediately relinquished all hope and collapsed into whimpering terror. Eva insulted her trembling lover, finally having to push him off into the night with his police escort. In exile fear so paralyzed Perón that he could not bear to sleep alone in the dark. Eva, in contrast, neither weakened nor vacillated as she began her crusade through the streets of Buenos Aires to save her man.

When the great day of October 17 arrived, a dauntless Eva again had to force Juan Domingo into action, dragging him onto the balcony of the House of Government so that the workers could acclaim him as their saviour.

Eva's lack of confidence in Perón grew after their marriage. She manoeuvred the appointment of her brother as her husband's private secretary: through Juancito she controlled the audiences and activities of the President. Later, when Perón's conflict with the church flared, Eva, as a good and sincere Roman Catholic, loyally undermined the régime's machinations against the church.

The political and personal conflict within the ruling couple surfaced during Eva's brief candidacy for the vice-presidency and her subsequent renunciation. At this point Perón frustrated her hopes of supplanting him. Her decline in health followed, becoming so marked that it put an end to her ambitions as well as to the First Lady's active opposition to her husband. Nevertheless, she took control for one last time during the abortive revolution of September 1951. At the first sign of danger, Perón took refuge in the Brazilian embassy, but Eva hunted him down and dragged him back to the defence of his people.

Finally, she could no longer move from her bed. Perón rejoiced, not only as he watched a major threat to his power removed, but also as he realized that the Lady of Hope served him better sick than in good health. He forced her to accompany him according to the needs of his electoral campaign with no consideration for the suffering this could cause her. The pleas of her doctors to let her rest only infuriated him. For the inaugural parade of his second term, the President tied his dying wife to a special apparatus in his open car.

Later, as her condition worsened, Perón continued to use Evita's suffering as the focus for mass demonstrations of solidarity with the régime. But revolted by the odours and moans which issued from her room, he could not bear to comfort her. At last, in his irritation, her husband arranged an operation on Eva's brain, silencing the cries of pain which so annoyed him. Having reduced her to insensibility he began clandestinely to remove her perfumes and jewels, destined later for the hands of his adolescent lovers, to another residence.

With Eva dead and her embalmed corpse in his hands, Perón

proceeded to manipulate her image solely for his own self-aggrandise-
ment. He had announced that he would replace Eva in her work in
the Ministry of Labour and Welfare, but showing neither conviction
nor energy, went to her desk only three times, whining that the work
tired him. In collusion with the labour syndicates, the widower began
to plot the future of Eva's body, which he had preserved for purposes
of propaganda. After its display in the capital, Perón intended to
parade the coffin and its valuable contents through the provinces,
marshalling support for his régime.

The Liberating Revolution of the anti-Peronists destroyed these
macabre projects, wresting from unworthy hands the remains of the
valiant woman with whom all good had disappeared from Peronism.
Saving her from the degradation of an eternal circus sideshow, the
military gave Eva Perón the honour which was her due. Those who
kidnapped the body in 1955 did so in order to bury her in standing
position, a traditional tribute rendered warriors in death, honouring
her as eternally unvanquished. 'She is standing!' shouted the
colonel.[16] 'I buried her standing, like Facundo, because she was a
macho!'

5
Preliminary Analysis

A pattern surfaces in the images of the Lady of Hope and the woman of the Black Myth. The praises of one and the accusations of the other both concern sexuality, femininity, taste and education, and association or mystic rapport with the masses: elements of the population thought to be least assimilated into and controlled by the established order of culture and civilization as middle class Argentinians know it. Orthodox Peronism lauded Eva Perón as the incarnation of a feminine ideal; anti-Peronism denounced her as the negation of that very ideal. For orthodox Peronism the appearance and graces, contacts, culture, and possessions necessary to a certain social status put the finishing touches on her image of unimpeachable femininity. In anti-Peronist eyes, she had spent her entire life motivated by a futile struggle to obtain precisely the same status symbols. The Lady of Hope received her due in tribute to her spiritual leadership paid her by the populace of Argentina who, childlike and uncorrupted by learning and formal ideologies, had intuitively turned to their Evita. The woman of the Black Myth exploited the blind response to her demagoguery of gullible, primitive Peronist masses. From the panegyric of one myth and the contumely of the other emerge the same underlying values.

THE WOMAN

The feminine nature emerging from the images of the Lady of Hope and the woman of the Black Myth [1] is one defined in terms of physical drives and instincts, emotions, and appropriate roles. As such, ideal femininity is irrational, its physical and emotional essence rendering it a source of power that transcends the bounds of protocol, rules, or reason itself. When the physical and emotional bases of this power are controlled, the myths accord it a positive value; they assess it negatively when emotion, intuition, and physical drives exercise their influence uncurbed.

The Peronist myth established links between the Lady of Hope and her specifically female physical and emotional nature. She is above all wife and mother. But her conjugal love is chaste, and her maternal love, childless. This woman's roles are defined in terms of her physical nature, yet she never surrenders unrestrainedly to her physical drives. The theme of her purity reiterates this: the female sexuality of the Lady of Hope is present, but controlled. The quality of chastity is important to an Eva who attracts followers through a saintly magnetism. Similarly, she exercises a maternal role as moral and spiritual guardian. Her feminine emotionality under the aegis and control of Juan Domingo Perón inspires intuitive and mystical loyalities that define her very special type of leadership as complementary to the institutionalized and "scientific" leadership of her husband. In these senses, her female sexuality, in its controlled form, fits her for spiritual power.

The woman of the Black Myth gives herself up entirely to her emotional and intuitive impulses, above all complying and colluding with the dictates of her sex drive. Sex dominates this Eva, and she dominates others through it. This accounts not only for her power over Perón himself and over her adherents in government circles; her enemies sometimes insinuated that an erotic element was closely connected with Eva's sway over her mass following. The masses either associated their enthusiasm for her with their physical impulses, or the attraction she exercised over them was in part sexual. Meanwhile, her emotions and intuitions, far from controlled, were given free rein by Perón, reaching paroxysms of sentimental passion and violence. In all this, while refusing the roles of dependent wife and devoted mother, Evita reversed the ideal order in which a woman's physical and emotional nature remains under control.

Beauty, Purity, and Femininity
Woman, as she exists in the world depicted by the Peronist media, is by definition beautiful. 'Woman Peronists', confided a leader of the Feminine Branch of Peronism, 'always preserve their femininity.

They take great care of their appearance.'[2] Femininity is beauty, but it is beauty of a certain kind. Eva captivated orthodox Peronism with a blond loveliness that was delicate and fragile, slight and girlish. The finely drawn lines of her face and body told of weakness, belying her fortitude, both physical and spiritual. 'This was the importance of Eva's appearance,' explained the same woman leader. 'All were amazed to see a woman of such beauty with a spirit of such strength.' But Eva did not possess this fragility alone among women; it marks the female sex, typifying all womanly beauty.[3] Eva herself, through *La razón de mi vida*, stated, 'I know that, like every woman of the people, I have more strength than I appear to have'.[4]

Peronist propaganda easily associated this particular type of physical appearance and its connotations of the slender maiden which Eva Perón began to cultivate soon after becoming First Lady of Argentina with the idea of physical and spiritual purity. Eva maintained her tiny figure with difficulty[5] and possibly, even probably, did so as many women do for reasons of fashion. But the media controlled by the party played down the significance of Eva's personal motives and did not allow these motives to enter into her public image.

Official Peronism insisted on the association of Eva Perón with the idea or signs of sainthood or, often more specifically, of the Virgin Mary. 'She's just like the Virgin!' exclaimed a little girl from the provinces described in pro-Peronist literature long before Eva's death.[6] After her death, Peronists made this claim with increasing frequency. A plaque in memory of the deceased First Lady showed a halo surrounding her head, and the press description of its unveiling proclaimed Evita '*Madona de América*'.[7] Illustrations in state school books also circled the well-known features in their austere frame of blonde hair with an aureole, the nimbus sometimes taking the form of a cross.[8] A labour union emphasized similar themes yet again on a sheet printed in the form of a devotional leaflet: the halo, the traditional pose, the blue and white robes are those of Mary. But the classic veil frames the unmistakeable face of Eva Perón.[9]

Yet, in the orthodox Peronist image of Eva, this femininity, with its emphasis on purity, assumes its deepest importance and highest dignity in its aspects of wife and mother. Peronists sometimes join the themes of sexual purity and a conjugal relationship by stressing the irreproachable fidelity of Eva Perón to her husband. They pointedly disregard her life before marriage. The Eva Perón of *La razón de mi vida* and *Historia del Peronismo* goes so far as to suggest, if not a sexless marriage, a careful muting of sex, a sacrifice that allowed Eva and Juan better to dedicate themselves to their people. Eva's followers sometimes reiterate this theme by affirming that Juan and Eva Perón did not sleep together. They base this idea either on the different schedules of husband and wife or on the widespread knowledge that during the last years of her life, Eva's illness prevented her from having sexual relations with her husband. Far from the scorn expressed by anti-Peronists when they relate the same circumstances, admiration dominates in the Peronist version, in which Eva sacrificed her sex life along with her health in the course of her increasing dedication to her people.

But to the anti-Peronist mind, Eva Perón's appearance suggests, far from physical or spiritual purity, her sexuality. Her enemies dwell on the Eva of the years preceding her husband's assumption of power and her first three years as First Lady. Not only did she display her most flamboyant toilettes during this period, but at the same time Eva verged on a plumpness that anti-Peronists view as evidence of her voluptuousness.

They recount the nature of the sexual habits and appetites of 'La Duarte' in detail,[10] seldom doubting that Eva indulged in prostitution as a profession and that her efforts as an actress feebly disguised this fact. Some portray her as the owner of a brothel herself. Even so internationally respected a figure as Jorge Luis Borges cites this as a major factor in the motivation of both Peróns:[11]

> And his wife was a common prostitute. She had a brothel near Junín. And that must have embittered him, no? I mean, if a girl is a whore in a large city that doesn't mean too much, but in a small town in the pampas, everybody knows everybody else. And being one of the whores is like being the barber or the surgeon. And that must have greatly embittered her. To be known and to be despised by everybody and to be used.

Condemning the occasion on which Evita met her future husband, an anti-Peronist version displays contempt: 'It was a dance, a party, a Bacchanal'.[12]

So evident is the paramount position granted Eva Perón's sexual immorality within the anti-Peronists' Black Myth that even they could not fail to notice it. While Perón was still in power an opponent of his régime remarked that fellow members of the opposition claimed that they objected to Eva because of her political role, but that the specific criticisms seemed always to take the form of gossip about her scandalous past. 'Their murmurings attributed to her a licence difficult to imagine and impossible to resist by any feminine constitution.'[13] The anti-Peronist concern to damn Eva Perón's dissolute sex life manifests a preoccupation with sexual purity equal to that seen in the Peronist emphasis on her chastity. The positive values usually implied by the exaggerated anti-Peronist criticism of Eva's physical vices surface in a typical affirmation that

> tyranny, persecution, the confiscation of goods and even the worst evils which dictatorships provoke can be supported; but it is impossible to tolerate moral rotteness . . . Perón could not take away . . . the ancient right which a country holds to the modesty, the virginity, and the purity of its women.[14]

Although for many anti-Peronists the early promiscuity or prostitution of Evita Duarte sufficed to brand her forever, some of the tales circulated by her enemies accuse her of continuing her questionable practices after marriage, although 'on a very high level, corresponding with her position'.[15] Other anti-Peronist versions of Eva's history, paradoxically, negate not only her morality but her sexuality in the forms necessary to the role of respectable wife. These versions described her as frigid, or tending toward frigidity. Eva and Juan, in these accounts, found each other attractive precisely because they were alike in their lack of sexuality. So reprehensible a basis for a relationship could only have equally lamentable results: husband and wife did not sleep together.

The Wife

The honoured roles of wife and mother demand that the identity of the woman fuse with that of her husband.

The total dependence of women on men results in part from their quintessential frailty, and in part from the obedience of virtuous womanhood in all things to the dictates, not of reason or the mind, but of emotion and the heart. Eva and Juan prepared for marriage and power, he, knowing well what he wanted to do; I, only feeling it; he, with the intelligence; I, with the heart; he, prepared for the struggle; I, ready for everything without knowing anything; he cultured and I simple; he, enormous, and I, tiny; he, the master, and I, the student. He, the figure and I the shadow... He, sure of himself and I, sure only of him![16]

Any apparent initiative or exercise of rational faculties on the part of a truly feminine woman is in fact due to emotion: it expresses her love for a man.

When Eva as new wife and First Lady began to visit factories, the workers received her enthusiastically. The media carefully defined their response: 'The presence of Señora Perón always causes joy amongst the descamisados of the nation precisely because this presence is considered that of her husband'. 'In their hearts, the workers now unite the figure of María Eva Duarte de Perón with that of the revolutionary leader.'[17]

Although the Peronist press later gave indications of a role for Eva independent of Juan Perón, throughout her life Eva herself in speeches and in *La razón de mi vida* continued to claim that her leadership and her personality were ultimately and completely identified with those of her husband. The press, too, reverted to this theme after the death of the First Lady, publicizing attempts to substitute Juan Perón for Eva Perón in all the areas where her loss might be considered irreparable. 'What miracle is this, ... that Eva Perón is also Juan Perón, and Juan Perón is also Eva Perón?' 'He is giving us the most complete definition of Evita, the only definition possible: Evita was the perfect manifestation of Perón.'[18]

In the process of re-identifying himself with his deceased wife, Perón returned to 'the glorious secretariat' of Labour and Welfare, and to his former self: Colonel Perón. Evita had invoked the work of the 'old Colonel Perón' in the Secretariat as the precedent of her role in the new Ministry; now, seven years later, Perón in turn invoked the endeavour of his wife as the basis for his re-assumption of his own former tasks, as well as of roles unique to Eva.[19]

Eva refused, in the anti-Peronist view, to assume the secondary role that every woman should accept, particularly in her move into the position of wife. Except in versions based on transformations occurring after her death, the Black Myth inveighs against Eva Perón as the dominant member in the presidential marriage. Anti-Peronists deplore her presentation of herself as an important source of initiative within the government itself, but they brand as even worse the fact that this initiative arose from personal ambitions. Her husband figured, if at all, as no more than another means to her ends. But, notably, her enemies do not specifically criticize these ends or the content of Eva's political or personal initiatives, although they sometimes vaguely condemn both as expressions of excessive lust for power.

Anti-Peronists aimed their contempt, then, less at the goals of Eva's action than at the action itself. Her enterprise negated the passivity and dependence considered virtuous in womankind. In her refusal to play a traditional female role, Eva Perón rejected the modest, domestic, submissive, and dependent identity that is necessary in a woman dedicated to providing the appropriate background for the man who dominates her and her life. Versions of the Black Myth frequently and explicitly contrast Eva's life with the expectations of this traditional role, condemning her in terms of the same ideal that Peronist mythology used to extol her.

The Mother

Next in importance to her love for her husband, according to orthodox Peronism, Eva's love for the common people of her country impelled her to enter the political arena. She felt and expressed this devotion as interchangeable with, if not identical to, a motherly devotion. The orthodox Peronist interpretation of popular enthusiasm for the Evita of the masses held that they felt towards their 'Standard Bearer' an effusive and irrational love that might be attributed to children: 'Love felt by the people is a strong sentiment . . . it runs blindly toward its object and then becomes calm, like the sea which calms itself after its tremendous battle with the elements'.[20]

Peronist descriptions of Eva as the perfect mother place great importance within the role of motherhood on the duties of a woman as teacher and protector of her children. It is woman's role as the chief agent responsible for the transmission of the values that uphold society as a whole that gives her position in the home its paramount value.

> Her task must be carried out equally in all areas: in the shop, in the office, in the laboratory, in the Peronist headquarters [*unidad básica*] of her neighborhood, and above all, in the place where her presence is the link of love and the custodian of faith: at the family table, the sounding box of the nation.[21]

Eva Perón, '*madre tutelar*' or '*alma tutelar*', provided the source of moral value and spiritual content within the Peronist movement. As such, she supplied a model for other mothers in their essential position as the transmitters of social and moral values from one generation to another.[22] Defined predominantly in these terms, her role of motherhood continued, needing no modification or reformulation, when death removed her physical presence.

A formulation of feminine nature as a source not only of physical nurturing but also of moral guidance gives added meaning to Eva Perón's social work and the interpretation of much of her action in such other fields as labour. The first workers whom Evita received in the Secretariat of Labour and Welfare, according to the régime's propaganda, arrived at her desk to donate funds and clothes for the poor. Eva's efforts in social welfare proved her special links with the labouring classes: her 'programme distinguished her as a sincere friend of the people, and especially, of the workers for whom she feels true affection'.[23] In this area Eva could carry out activities that remained taboo in the field of politics. More than a year before official reports defined her participation in the First Governors' Conference as limited to the role of auditor, the First Lady herself called and presided over a meeting of the governors and federal interveners of all the provinces, the ministers of Public Works and of Finance, the Mayor of Buenos Aires, and the president of the Central Bank of the Argentine Republic as part of a conference on the housing projects of her Foundation.[24]

Political motives could have accounted in part for the omission from publicity of Eva's more directly political action. But by disregarding this facet of her activity, Peronist propaganda may have better fitted her image to an ideal of womanhood in which a maternal role is paramount. Eva herself announced 'More than political action, the women's movement needs to carry out social action. Precisely because social action is something which we women carry in our blood'.[25]

The physical and spiritual aspects of motherhood and of social work involve another typically feminine role: the woman as sentinel, standing guard not only over the material resources necessary for the care of her family but over domestic morality as well. When economic difficulties began for the régime, the housewife was assigned a specific role in the defense of the national budget. Eva Perón proclaimed that 'Each Peronist woman will be, in the heart of her home, the sentinel of austerity, avoiding waste, diminishing consumption and increasing production'. The housewife had become the 'mistress of the national destiny'.[26]

Outside the domestic realm, the characteristic vigilance of the Peronist woman assumed a political role. In this capacity, her feminine nature qualified her for a unique place in 'the struggle against betrayal'. Her surveillance of the domestic economy and morality militated in a larger sphere 'against anything which might be the seed of destruction; against the flattery and temptations which the capitalist oligarchy and foreign imperialisms attempt to use in order to reach their goals'. And Eva Perón, the model of the protective nature of Peronist womanhood, took on the role of special defender of her husband and his works.[27]

The Black Myth denies Eva's maternal proclivities, but less strongly than the image of the Lady of Hope stresses them. The emphasis placed by anti-Peronists on Eva Perón's sexual immorality, her lack of domesticity, and her dominant and aggressive nature renders unnecessary further attacks on the motherly portrait painted by the Peronists. The failures of 'that woman' in areas of essential femininity virtually eliminate the question of her success or failure as a mother: the anti-Peronist who has just finished the usual list of scabrous anecdotes about Eva's career as a prostitute scarcely feels it necessary to proceed to explain why she was considered an unmotherly figure. The listener himself would not await clarification of reasons for doubts about the maternal instinct of a person who wears fur coats and gives speeches over the radio instead of staying home to knit, cook, and bake cakes.

Nevertheless, the Black Myth negates in some ways the Peronist claims of Evita's motherly nature. Among these are the suggestions of her frigidity and even sterility. During Eva's long periods of illness, an extreme and now extinct account arose, denying in a dramatically different way her possession of any sincere motherly love. Women of the aristocratic, and therefore anti-Peronist, neighbourhood of Barrio Norte whispered that Eva needed fresh blood to recuperate, and that the sick woman had ordered the blood extracted from children. Frightened mothers of the area warned each other not to take their children to hospitals or pharmacies, where they supposed the macabre orders were carried out.[28]

In the process of discrediting Eva's efforts at social aid, her enemies portray her as devoid of any maternal instinct or sentiment. Anti-Peronists deride as hypocrisy the love for children that Eva herself so often vaunted. They dismiss all the institutions for which she took the credit as no more than deceptive façades, set up only for the sake of Eva's ambition. Eva's alleged failure in this area assumes particular significance when considered within the context of the place of social aid in the lives of Argentinian women. The highly prestigious *Sociedad de Beneficiencia* had carried out social work in Argentina for over a century. For this task it drew its members from the paragons of Argentinian femininity among the nation's upper classes. Circles and classes other than their own shared the high opinion of these women and their labours. Their work became a badge of feminine honour: they could offer the presidency of the society as a privilege to the wife of each Argentinian President. This was so until Eva Duarte de Perón stood waiting for the traditional prerogative. And her critics deemed Eva Duarte de Perón, even before she demonstrated her own personal style of social aid, which later scandalized them, incapable of this task, which belonged only to the finest of Argentinian womanhood.

The Martyr

Woman's passivity is virtually complete in her roles as wife and mother. In the world of the Peronist myth she willingly and even happily undertakes abnegation and sacrifice, recognizing this as the only way to her true self-fulfillment. The capacity to *give* and to *give up* are basic to the nature of womanhood. Eva had accepted, her autobiography stated, the role of victim and of slave, but never had she felt so free as when subjected to the will and personality of Juan Domingo Perón.[29] In the Renunciation, the refusal of the vice-presidency, and her premature death, Eva's love for the humble and poor of her nation soon transcended even an exalted and altruistic passion to reach the height of martyrdom, according further grounds for the reverence and loyalty of the people, who saw her as their spiritual example and guide.

The entire theme of the Renunciation and the emphasis laid on Eva's premature death, while not due only to this factor, figure importantly in the idea of Eva Perón as exemplary of the essence of womanhood.[30] Ideas of her sacrifice formed part of her image long before her followers could have foreseen the possibility of her death. The theme began to insinuate itself into the reports of the press even when knowledge of the seriousness of her disease had not yet been made public. After her first operation, which these reports describe as an appendectomy, *Democracia* suggested that 'one must not disregard the possibility that all would have been easier and more bearable had Señora Perón dedicated more attention . . . to her own health problems than to the . . . tasks of social aid which she had imposed upon herself'.[31] After the Renunciation and her death, the theme of martyrdom appears explicitly linked to both, allowing them as sacrifices to merge as acts of similar quality.[32]

The element of renunciation carries particular force in the Argentinian context by virtue of its precedent in the life of San Martín. Argentinians remember as bitterly difficult sacrifices both San Martín's decision to leave international leadership to Simón Bolivar and his refusal to involve himself in the internal political strife of his country, preferring exile. Perón himself mentions the importance of sanmartinian renunciation as early as 1948, while régime propaganda later praised the same quality in the attitude of the leader. The press also referred to this tradition when describing the famous Day of Renunciation of Eva Perón.[33]

During Eva's final illness and after her death the mouthpieces of orthodox Peronism continued to interpret the course of events as a conscious sacrifice of her life for her people: 'Who knows if her intuitive wisdom had not announced to her her premature end?' 'The prolonged effort, that prodigality without limits, that enthusiasm for the resolution of all the problems, small and large, of an infinity of beings, had undermined her organism.' Union speeches and declarations of solidarity with official mourning echoed the journals' main themes in the days following the death.[34]

The ideas of renunciation, sacrifice, and martyrdom by association implied the concept of sainthood. This at least was the reasoning of *Democracia*. The words 'Santa Evita' appeared for the first time in connection with the day dedicated to Eva Perón in recognition of her selfless renunciation of the vice-presidency. The newspaper made little use of this title, which it took care to attribute to other sources, although these were in at least one case anonymous.[35]

If the exact words were not employed, other expressions and facts used in the press suggested similar concepts. Some of the titles conferred upon Evita Perón during this period may even have found a precedent in *Democracia's* own early epithet, The Lady of Hope. After the announcement of 'Saint Evita Day' and just before her death, *Democracia* reported the bestowal upon the ailing First Lady of two titles that may easily have possessed saintly overtones: 'The Spiritual Chief of the Nation' and 'Spiritual Protector of the Argentinian University'.[36]

To the anti-Peronists, Eva, who had been incapable of accepting a properly passive femininity in her relationship with Juan Perón, could scarcely give a credible performance in the role of martyr on the larger scale of public life. If she expended herself on behalf of the Argentinian people, they said, she did so with her own interests uppermost in her mind. As early as 1946, her enemies accused her of ambitions of becoming Argentina's first woman senator. Later they expressed similar suspicions of the real nature of Señora Perón's vital interest in the field of women's suffrage: 'Is this a form of mobilizing the women with a definite end which could well be to increase and reinforce the constituency for a lady with aspirations to be a candidate? History will tell'.[37] Anti-Peronism had few doubts that Eva's followers accorded her a position of saint and madonna by virtue of their belief in her sacrifices for them. But in actuality, her opponents believed, Eva did not seek the position of a Queen of Heaven so much as one which would be 'slightly more than what a queen might be in an absolute monarchy'.[38]

STATUS SYMBOLS

Both the orthodox Peronist myth and the Anti-Peronist myth of Eva Perón reveal certain elements as important symbols of status and acceptance in the world and society they depict. Both versions positively value and heavily accentuate contacts with the upper classes, an appearance characteristic of them, material possessions considered to be their prerogative, and a level of education recognized in language and in knowledge of general European culture and art: the signs of civilization. Their absence sentences individuals or entire groups to barbarism.

The difference here between the two renditions of the image of Evita parallels the differences that have been indicated in the cases of all elements examined to this point. The Peronist version claims that Eva enjoyed rights to the contacts and possessions, and that she was endowed with the appropriate education. The anti-Peronists maintain that much of Eva's life was dedicated to attempts to obtain these status symbols and the concomitant recognition within established society, but that she failed completely in these attempts. Both place similar value on the symbols, but the Peronists praise Eva for her ability to obtain and manipulate them while the anti-Peronists mock her for her failure to do so. When, however, either party recognizes these symbols of social position in the possession of members of the opposition, it generally discredits the possessor on ideological grounds or in terms of mere ostentation. Although the symbols are valued in themselves, it considered wrong for a person whose true nature does not merit it to enjoy the social distinction they denote.

In both myths, then, Eva lays claims to tastes, possessions, and contacts that symbolize the social status to which she aspires, and both concern themselves centrally with these claims, one endeavouring to establish and the other to destroy them. But the different images do more than associate Eva with determined social sectors. Generally speaking, refinement of manner and taste, possessions that testify to such discrimination, and social contacts themselves are intimately related to the concept of culture or civilization. They are, further, believed to be the result not of learning but of inborn sensitivity to the spiritual as against the material and physical aspects of existence. By arrogating the symbols of social status Eva Perón could identify herself as part of civilization as mainstream Argentinian culture had defined it. Further, she, as representative of members of the popular Peronist following with the most despised social standing, could claim for them the same identity. If she could make it, then so also could they.

But if Eva could not make good her claims, as the Black Myth insisted she could not, the links with civilization that she laboured vainly to forge for herself and her followers could never hold. They had no rights to the symbols of culture and no place in the realm for which they stood. Prisoners of their physical drives and gross material interests, with no sign of innate higher sensibility, Eva and Peronism found themselves outside the longed-for world of civilization, and were defined as barbarians.

Here an important qualification must be made. Rational control of the realms of the physical and emotional, like the status symbols just mentioned, is also inextricably related to the idea of culture or civilization. However, such rationality is explicitly attributed to men. Women, in contrast, glory in their intuitive and emotional approach to life, although accepting the fact that it must be controlled—usually, directly or indirectly, by men.

Further, Argentinians implicitly establish a special relationship between ideal femininity and these status symbols. Feminine beauty is defined as both delicate and elegant. Its delicacy implies not only a refinement of body but of manner: the bearing thought to be characteristic of high social position. A beautiful woman's elegance exhibits not only physical attractiveness but grooming and possessions that enhance and adorn that attractiveness according to a standard of fashion. The fluctuations of this standard, further, demand continuous investment. Finally, Argentinians identify as a feminine domain culture, education, and sensitivity to the concinnities of language and especially to the arts. Taste as involving values central to society becomes a form of virtue. A congruence emerges between woman's role as guardian and transmitter of a culture's morality and her role as protectress of aesthetic standards and patroness of the arts.

Versions of the official myth of Eva Perón, contradicting other areas of Peronist propaganda—which denounce both social distinctions and the dominant Argentine social classes—use social distinctions as convenient and correct categories for description, and often comment positively on Eva's association with elements of the European upper classes. This is especially true in descriptions carried by the press of Eva's tour of Europe in 1947. The commentary and the emphasis it received through repetition and accompanying photographs suggests that the social hierarchy represented by the aristocracy with which the press showed Eva Perón to consort constitutes a positive value in the world depicted by orthodox Peronist propaganda.

Eva's followers expressed their conviction that unbiased circles of cultivated society, in this case necessarily outside Argentina, would readily and naturally accept their leader by describing Eva as '*fina*', referring not only to her physical delicacy or to the fineness of the lines and construction of her face and body. In Argentinian Spanish the word '*fina*' implies as well the impression of fine quality as does its equivalent in English when applied to goods. When used to describe a woman, the word generally has social connotations. An Argentinian understands a *mujer fina* to be delicate of body and, even more importantly, of gesture. But above all, a *mujer fina* is capable of moving in, and being appreciated by, cultivated society. An association between beauty and class in this sense becomes explicit. A wealthy Peronist made this association unmistakeable when, in an interview, he described an experience from a party barbecue: He had been sitting by the swimming pool when he noticed a young woman coming out of the water. Her lovely [*linda*] face and lovely [*lindo*] body so struck him that he enquired who she might be. 'Imagine my surprise', he reminisced, 'when they told me that she was the wife of a labour leader! That shows you how much Argentina has changed since the first days of Peronism.'[39]

In this context, the epithet *'señoras gordas'*, used by the Peronists to designate the rich women of the opposition, may have implications beyond the association of corpulence with wealth. Obesity itself functions as a contradiction of the feminine ideal and invalidates claims to class superiority and to its concomitant high level of culture. This is only one element in the meaning of this expression, but one that may account in part for its insulting nature.

Social contacts and hierarchy, as mentioned above, are equally important in the anti-Peronist myth of Eva Perón. In one of its major themes, the Black Myth derides Eva's efforts to ascend to the revered heights of the accepted social scale. It shows her envy of those on levels higher than hers not only as the motivation for her attempts to rise within the social herarchy, but also as the driving force behind her entire political and personal life. The myth dwells on her early attempts to enter the Argentinian upper classes, scoffs at the alleged movements of the 'Presidenta' amongst figures of European society, and scorns both Eva's failure to attain the social status she sought and the bitter vengefulness this failure caused, manifested in persecution of the women who held precisely the social positions the First Lady coveted.

By emphasizing Eva's early image, which was plumper and sexually suggestive, the anti-Peronists negate the Peronist definition of Evita as a *mujer fina*. They may often admit her prettiness, but they then qualify it as common or vulgar. Throughout her life, some state, even when she had finally attained the svelte and classic appearance of her later years, her enemies could detect her origins in the gutter. She could never hide the fact that she was basically a coarse woman with heavy bones that no diet could reduce or refine. This stigma casts doubt on her natural endowments and converts the spectacular Eva of her last years to the artificial result of the money and time that her vanity demanded and her new position permitted her to cultivate.

Both images of Eva Perón depict amongst her material possessions those that symbolized certain position within the 'society' which they value. And in both, there are elaborately detailed accounts of the First Lady's wardrobe, which eclipsed all her other belongings, throwing them into the shadow of the splendour of her dress. The continuing centrality of Eva's clothes in the myths reflects their importance in establishing her claims to ideal feminity not only through her beauty but through her elegance. In other words, she asserted this claim in terms of the congruence of her features with the ornaments which adorned them. But 'Although the monkey dresses herself like a lady', say the Argentinians, 'she continues to be a monkey'.

The Peronist press railed against the 'haughty ladies of Barrio Norte' as synonymous with the 'ladies of the oligarchy'. But a popular cartoon history of Eva Perón stated with satisfaction that when the young actress Eva Duarte first tasted prosperity she installed herself in an apartment in the elegant barrio of these same ladies. While Eva herself made in her speeches scornful references to the ladies of the oligarchy with their pedigree lapdogs, official Peronism accepted her own pedigree poodles as so associated with her image that they appeared in the régime's school texts as well as in the form of bejewelled miniatures on a gold bracelet that Congress offered its First Lady as a gift.[40]

Once again the trip to Europe, in itself a luxury reserved for the oligarchy, served as an excuse for inventories of the trunkloads of gifts that Eva brought home with her and for even more elaborate descriptions of the wardrobe with which she dazzled the Europeans. While the gifts have for the most part been forgotten in the ensuing years, Eva's spectacular elegance and its sartorial details still figure importantly in her myth.

Over the years orthodox Peronism has continued to stress Eva Perón's dress, defining it as congruent with an ideal of general feminine elegance. At the time of the trip to Europe, the details of her clothing occupied a central place in the pro-Peronist newspaper reports of each day's activities. After her death, a text for second graders said of her that 'Once upon a time, there was a blonde woman, delicate and elegant, like story-book princesses'.[41] These specific descriptions and emphasis on detail again point up the special significance of this elegance. Eva's beauty and her dress help to lay the sometimes militant and sometimes unconscious claim of some Peronists to one of the defining characteristics of the Argentine upper classes. Recent propaganda by elements of Peronism considered to represent orthodox and bureaucratic sectors of the party asserted this claim in the caption to a photograph of Eva in an elaborate evening gown: 'She could dazzle like a queen—a thing which the oligarchy never forgave her—but she continued to be one of the people. And this was even less pardonable'.[42]

The Black Myth, like the orthodox Peronist propaganda, emphasizes Eva's accumulation of luxuries. But it interprets these as part of her unsuccessful attempt to compete socially with her enemies by displaying the material symbols of their rank. Also like its Peronist counterpart, the anti-Peronist myth concentrates, amidst references to other possessions, on the wardrobe of Eva Perón.

Anti-Peronists sometimes rationalize their emphasis on the former First Lady's clothes by pointing out the contrast between Eva's alleged position as benefactress of the 'shirtless ones' and her own very well-adorned self. The epithet for the Peronist masses makes the contradiction a very obvious one, but it does not seem enough to account for the emphasis given the paradox by the anti-Peronist Right. In fact the same paradox appears to have passed unnoticed by this sector on other occasions in Argentinian history. No one, for example, levelled such widespread criticism at the extravagant costume parties or gala balls held by different charitable organizations in Argentina to benefit the poor. To the Right, this mode of dress represents a positively valued distinction of class to which Eva had no claim.

For some of the anti-Peronist Left at the time of the first Peronist régime, the contradiction lay between the Peróns' criticisms of the upper classes as decadent and Eva's adoption of one of the identifying marks of those classes: their elegant dress. To the Left this elegance symbolizes the dissipation against which Eva claimed she was protesting, and proves her insincerity. However, this element in the censure of Eva Perón by the Left has existed in the context of other elements, in particular those related to descriptions of the popular following of Peronism, which manifest a lesser ingredient of a leftist ethic and a

The plates represent the types of visual images which the Argentinians find familiar and which they associate with the different myths of Eva Perón

This page
THE ACTRESS

Above
THE FIRST LADY
The typical salute of Eva and Juan Perón

Right
THE SOCIAL WORKER
The desk in Labour and Welfare
THE MOTHER

EVA THE PRESIDENT'S WIFE

EVA OF LA RAZON DE MI

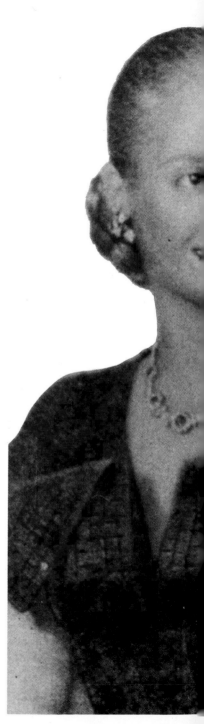

EVA THE INCENDIARY

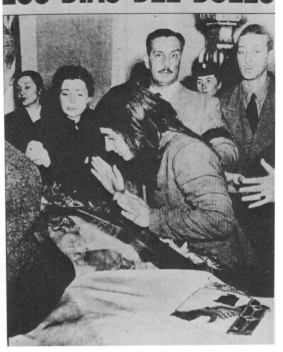

LOS DIAS DEL DUELO

EVA DE AMERICA
Madona de los Humildes

Angela Rina Rodríguez

St. Eva rises to the call of power

THIS surely must be he most bizarre, and macabre move ever made in international politics: the return of Eva Peron to the Argentine.

She is the last ace in the ack of her husband, ex-President **Juan Peron**. He as just gone back to the Argentine to stage his omeback after eighteen ears' exile in Madrid, riggering off riots which ... twenty dead on the treets.

He needs Eva more than anyone to back him up — for

Aires. Once on public show, Eva would revive memories of a better past, and rally the crowds to Peron.

Two relatives have reportedly travelled from the Argentine to remove the tattered remnants of the gown she was laid to rest in. She is now clothed in a dress especially designed by a Rome couturier. Her blonde hair has been carefully restyled in a chic, modern manner.

According to one top diplomatic source in Madrid: "She is beautifully preserved, but a strange sight to see in a person's home."

Eva Peron was once a music hall star.

Eva Peron—on show again.

hen they killed the Argentine, he was regarded virtually as saint by the adoring public.

But Eva died twenty-one ears ago from cancer. Peron as kept her with him in exile. mbalmed in a glass-topped offin.

For his trump card, Peron as had the body re-beautified or the public to see in the atin-lined coffin in Buenos

---

Opposite page
MADONNA AND MARTYR

Left
THE SAINT ABROAD
Ideas about women and women's power in many different cultures help explain why many people outside Argentina easily believe that Evita's people revered her as a saint. The opera *Evita* by Webber and Rice is the most spectacular evidence of the appeal of the saint abroad. (See Introduction; Chapter 1)

Below
THE WOMAN OF THE BLACK MYTH IN EUROPE
An anti-Peronist cartoonist portrays the King and Queen of England giving Eva and her "Hollywood-esque" style a cool reception

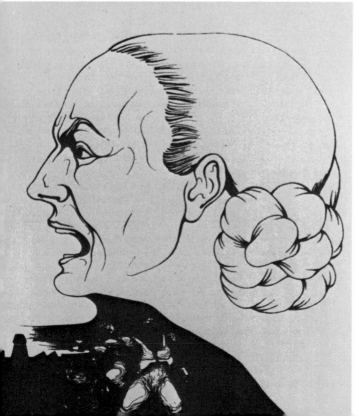

THE REVOLUTIONARY

Above
On the cover of a magazine of the Peronist Left

Below
The spark of controversy amongst different Peronist factions: Ricardo Carpani's drawing made Eva Perón 'ugly', according to some

greater emphasis on the values which coincide with those of the anti-Peronist Right.

The anti-Peronist myth, then, especially in versions of the Right, attacks more than an ideological inconsistency. It attempts to render Eva's claim to the garments she possesses invalid on the grounds of her social origins. It discredits as well any pretensions she might have had to native good taste. Eva's lack of taste, in anti-Peronist eyes, confirmed the inferiority of her social origins before she had the means and the experience to hide them and copy the Argentinian aristocracy. The Black Myth condemns the famous wardrobe not only for its extravagance but in terms of her original and permanent lack of refinement, repeatedly damning her taste as Hollywood-esque. This idea became a major theme of Copi's play 'Eva Perón', in which Evita planned for the display of her own corpse, carefully arranging to surround it with all her luxurious clothes in display cases. When she asked her mother for her opera dress, her mother replied that all her dresses were opera gowns. Copi himself stated that he presented Eva Perón as a Hollywood heroine because 'that was perhaps the only thing which she wanted to be and the only thing which she was denied'. [43]

Peronist and anti-Peronist descriptions of her talent and taste in the arts accentuate yet another element of the images of Eva Perón, distinguishing it as a special value in the universe they represent. Cultivation in this realm assumes a place on the list of dominant values found in these accounts. Significantly, Eva's husband gave no major indication of such interests.

This theme, even more than that of her wardrobe, continues a motif of Eva's earlier professional image. Publicity on the starlet Eva Duarte focused on her choice in works of art, her musical ability, and her taste in general. After her rise to power with her husband, these ideas again became important during her travels through Europe. News reports of her activities dwelt on her appreciation of the works that she made special trips to see. [44]

Later in her career, Eva Perón established a type of literary salon, or *peña*, known as the Peña Eva Perón, which received ample publicity over the years. This group met often at night after its patroness had finished her day's work, and still assumes importance in accounts of Eva's life. 'Eva Perón', some Peronists remember, 'gave herself time within her exhausting day's work to give her generous affection to poets, writers, and artists in general. She tried to communicate with them and maintained them close to her.'[45]

When one of Perón's followers amongst Argentinian university women turned against Eva, she chose to attack her in this area of culture, as manifested in general education and language: 'Since we have doctoral degrees, we can talk of Plutarch much better than she, and this bothers her. What Evita likes is to visit people of little culture, whom she astounds with recherché words'.[46]

The Black Myth derides Eva's lack of true knowledge and appreciation of the arts, making this theme a central one to its image. Anti-Peronists emphasize this and a series of parallel motifs, destroying any claims Eva Perón could make not only to artistic culture and taste, but to the most basic education and social manners. They lambaste her written and spoken language as incorrect, vulgar, profane, and inappropriate to the protocol of the situations in which her position placed her. These defects exercise an influence over anti-Peronist opinion that often equals that of major moral and political offences. A critic charged that Eva Perón lacked 'intelligence', knowledge of 'the moral and civil relations of men', 'autocriticism', and 'scruples of conscience'. He interspersed this list with other accusations undifferentiated from these in quality or importance: she also lacked 'culture' and 'feminine sensitivity', and, finally, she totally lacked 'taste'.[47]

THE MYSTIQUE AND THE MASSES

The orthodox Peronist and the anti-Peronist myths of Eva Perón contain similar definitions of her power. Both contain like descriptions of her mystique and of the reaction of her followers to it as purely emotional, similar in their irrational nature to her feminine sexuality. The two versions differ only in the values that they associate with this relationship between Evita and the popular masses of Peronism. Her attraction and their response were emotional, intuitive, mystic and, according to her enemies, even physical—in sum, irrational. After her death, according to both myths, these followers worshipped her in a cult, described by the Peronists as according her reverence as a saint or madonna at the side of the political ruler Perón, and portrayed by the anti-Peronists as pagan rites celebrated in honour of a usurping goddess.

Further, the association of Eva and popular Peronism related her to a set of people to whom, correctly or incorrectly according to differing points of view, marginal social status had traditionally been ascribed. Such a link specified her leadership as peripheral to the established forms of institutionalized power as well as to the rules and regulations of the society that had generated these institutions. Her special affinity for the *descamisados* in this context reiterated themes concerning the power of Eva Perón as uncontrolled in and of itself as well as irrational. Orthodox Peronism attributed the entire life of Eva Perón to a purely emotional type of motivation and mode of action. Her three loves, Perón, her country, and the anonymous masses of Argentina and the world, drove her ascent to power and the widening of her sphere of action. A few days before Argentinian women received the vote, an accomplishment considered Eva's, the régime's official mouthpiece honoured the patroness of the new legislation: 'The Lady of Hope/Is named Eva Duarte de Perón/The Lady of Hope/Is all emotion and heart'.[48]

As her career advanced, the press continued to explain her success in similar terms. In her ability to inspire the masses lay the most important political function of Eva Perón: exalted by her they transcended mere politics and converted Peronism into the redeeming crusade of a vast army.[49] She infused the increasingly monumental works of her Foundation for Social Aid with 'soul, . . . heart and . . . spirit', accounting for its achievements by claiming, 'We are not a Bureaucracy; on the contrary, we are a handful of persons working'.[50]

Eva's power differs dramatically in Peronist versions from that of her husband. Eva's style was impulsive, disordered, and emotive; her husband's, 'rigorous and scientific'.[51] Praises of Eva's disorganized way of working associated her disorder and unintellectual approach with her love for Perón and her people. Eva could express an emotional fanaticism for the Peronist cause. But Perón, who belonged to the military and thus to a profession that totally excluded women, is 'for that reason a friend of order and worked always with method and discipline', maintaining a respectable masculine equilibrium.[52]

The emotional content of the support that the nation seemed unconditionally to give its heroine contrasted with the political and bureaucratic structures and rules that restrict other public figures. When her party and people proclaimed Eva vice-president, the press announced, 'This is the second time in our political history—the only precedent being October 17, 1945—in which a candidacy has been formulated on the margin of all political procedure'. [53]

Anti-Peronism saw Eva in similar terms but translated them into the violence of dangerously uncontrolled energy and incendiary rhetoric, two fearful sources of her power. Early versions specifically accused the First Lady of personal responsibility for tortures carried out by the Perón régime. Her enemies continue to emphasize Eva's rages, often describing them as irrational seizures of passion or even insanity. [54]

Further, the opposition remembers clearly and with horror Eva's failure to understand the rules surrounding the formal life of a president's wife, or, if she understood them, her failure to use them. She mesmerized the masses with behaviour that violated all codes. Anti-Peronists still recall the repugnance they felt when a daring Eva arrived at a gala function in the Colón Opera House with her hair worn loose, in an era when, especially for formal occasions, women wore their hair caught up on their heads. The First Lady fascinated her followers but inspired only distaste in her enemies when, against all protocol, she occupied a place in the presidential coach. A military officer related a similar reaction to Eva when he glimpsed her arm over the back of Perón's chair while a minister took oath. This offence, to him, made her unbearable. [55]

Official Peronism's propaganda, because in general it addressed the Peronist populace, reflects its authors' definition of the working classes. The epithet of the Lady of Hope, with which the official press introduced the publicity campaign it dedicated to Eva Perón throughout her career, foreshadowed the basic features of the propaganda concerning Eva Perón, not only in the Peronist newspapers but in children's school texts and in the works attributed to the First Lady as well. Official Peronism portrayed Eva in vaguely religious or even specifically saintly terms, assuming that vast sectors of the Peronist public would be susceptible to such terms and to the ideas they represent and suggest. The creators of this orthodox propaganda presupposed that the masses would respond to this kind of suggestion, and formed a mystical cult around the party heroine.

Although titles such as the Lady of Hope, only the first of a series implying parallels to Christian hagiography, evidently have slightly sacrilegious connotations, they were immediately taken up whenever the opportunity arose. Raúl Apold emphatically denied the use of the term 'saint' in official organs, yet *Democracia* and other publications actually availed themselves of the word to designate Eva Perón,[56] often attributing the usage to other sources, in some cases anonymous. Although unwilling to risk the authorship of the idea, *Democracia* quoted *Le Monde*'s description of Eva Perón as a madonna of the Argentinian poor. The figure of speech was immediately seized as the title of a book of the same year: *Eva de América: Madona de los humildes*. Later, after Evita's death, a first grade reader repeated, 'She was a saint. And for that reason she flew to God'. In an illustration accompanying this text children gaze at a star in the form of a cross in the night sky. In still other books, Eva after death took her place by the side of God the Son, or on the right hand of God.[57]

Orthodox Peronism not only stated Eva's sainthood by directly using the word 'saint', but hinted at it as well, attributing to her the characteristics and functions of saints. Amongst these, her purity and her martyrdom, already elaborated here, figured importantly. Evita could also grant petitions, a power she evinced in her work in Labour and Welfare during her life and continued to exercise after her death, 'receiving' the letters of the poor through post boxes erected by the régime. Some versions introduce parallels with the lore of miracles such as those of Lourdes, recounting that Eva, after kissing the sore-encrusted mouth of a woman who appeared at her desk to request her aid, slapped a proffered bottle of disinfectant out of the hand of an assistant.[58]

In many of its frequent uses, the title Good Fairy referred to Evita's saintly nature and functions or linked her in other ways with formal religion. School texts and other Peronist literature connected Eva as a good fairy with angels and with her identity as saintly martyr. After her death the newspaper *La Razón* announced that "All the world mourns her, and God is at her side proclaiming her fairy, martyr, and saint'.[59] Argentinians do not commonly make a link between fairies and a religious realm. The link found in Peronist propaganda implies that the authors of such statements attributed a superstitious element to the religion of the mass public they hoped to reach.

The idea that the Argentinian masses felt a religious or mystical reverence for Eva Perón found explicit expression when *Democracia* attributed the identification of its leader as the Lady of Hope to the 'rare intuition' of the popular following of Peronism, which had transformed this image of Evita into a 'popular mystique'. The same concept was also implicit in the first description of Eva as a Madonna, which likened the crowds that poured into the Plaza de Mayo to see their Evita to the pilgrims arriving at the shrine of Lourdes. Propagandists could base their parallel on their qualification of the love of the people as uncontrollable, unreasoning, and blind. In such an interpretation, the popular sectors of Peronism reacted to phenomena and ideas not rationally, but with intuitive, emotional and even mystical responses such as those associated with religious fervour. 'It is easier for the people to love a man than to love a doctrine,' explained Eva Perón, 'because the humble people [*los pueblos*] are all heart.'[60]

This assumption helped to build a foundation in orthodox Peronism for confidence either in descriptions of prayers and promises of good conduct made to Evita by the Peronist masses, or in the ready reception by the public of such descriptions. First graders read 'Ave, Eva' on the first page of their reading texts below an illustration of Eva surrounded by angels. Second graders' texts began with the words of the little boy who, from the illustration on the first page, addressed the deceased First Lady: 'Our little mother, who art in heaven . . . Good Fairy who laughs amongst the angels . . . Evita: I promise you that I will be good'. At Eva's death, a children's magazine led its juvenile readership in a similar prayer:

> Evita, our love who art in Heaven, may your Goodness always accompany us. May you continue to protect our dreams and our games from the nearest star. May you continue to procure for us that which we may not have. May you continue to intercede before God the Father Almighty so that our elders may never lack fruitful work. May you continue to teach and guide our Fatherland, Free, Just, and Sovereign.[61]

Ideas of the religious connotations of mass adoration of Eva Perón's image also help to account for the emphasis of the Peronist press on the altars erected in the streets to the memory of Eva Perón. On the day following the end of Eva's struggle with cancer, the first page of *Democracia* announced that 'the image of Eva Perón is and will always be an object of intimate devotion' in the homes of the Argentinian nation. In subsequent weeks, the newspaper dedicated one full page of every edition to photographs and text on the subject of the altars raised and prayers offered in honour of Eva Perón.

Through this mouthpiece the régime affirmed that 'Those who have not been able to reach the room where the body lies in state have resignedly directed their steps toward the *unidades básicas* of the Women's Branch of the Peronist Party, and before the portait of Eva Perón they kneel down and pray, depositing floral offerings'. While 'an unending line passes before the altar raised in Plaza de Mayo . . . which is crowned by the portrait of Eva Perón', 'in many houses and seats of labour, political, and private associations, altars have been raised on which candles burn for the glorification of the woman who gave her all for her people'. Reports presented photographs and descriptions of altars in the *unidades básicas*, in unions, in private homes and in the streets. Articles transcribed prayers as well, depicting women in the street, before the altar in Plaza de Mayo, calling on Eva Perón as 'Regina Martirium . . . mater amabilis . . .' or as Santa Evita.[62]

When, toward the end of August, *Democracia*'s coverage of the mourning for Eva Perón began to diminish, an important change occurred: with no commentary whatsoever, articles began to designate the altars erected to the memory of the dead Evita, which to this point had been identified by the simple word '*altares*', as 'civic altars' [*altares cívicos*].[63] The change would seem to be a response to some pressure on the journalists to modify the unqualifiedly religious image which they had previously promoted. The idea of a cult of Eva and of the role of the altars in it still prevails in some sectors of Peronism today, demonstrating the continuing power of such an image.

However, the case of the altars strongly suggests that this idea, supported by orthodox Peronism, bases itself more on prejudice than on observation. Either consciously or unconsciously, this image omitted (and, even when edited, continued to omit) the indication of any connection between the altars constructed in honour of Eva Perón and those that form an apparently usual remembrance of the dead in many Argentinian homes, especially those in the lower socio-economic levels of society. Popular opinion and practice amongst groups where these altars exist associate them, and particularly the homage paid to the dead before them, only minimally with religion. Families may place photographs of deceased relatives on such an altar and offer prayers, but generally they pray in memory of the dead and not to them. Apparently, if people do not say prayers at the altar, they may treat it as a virtually completely secular memorial to the dead honoured there. Members of the working classes do mention the custom of addressing prayers to a dead person, but they describe such prayers in terms of requests for favours and not of cult rendered to the person addressed. Further, those who pray do not appear to associate this sort of petition with the home altars. In other words, out of ignorance or prejudice Peronist propaganda has either consciously distorted or unconsciously misinterpreted the phenomenon of the altars erected by the Peronist populace in memory of Evita.

The anti-Peronists' conviction that the image of Eva Perón attracted a 'cult of images which the commandments condemn'[64] demonstrates that their distortion of the evidence paralleled that of the Peronist myth-makers. Again, preconceptions about the nature of the Peronist masses and their relation to their patroness conditioned the anti-Peronist idea of such a cult. Like the authors of Peronist propaganda, they appear predisposed to believe that the street altars constituted proof that the popular masses literally worshipped their dead heroine, and necessarily either unconsciously ignore or consciously misrepresent or discard evidence concerning attitudes toward the dead amongst the Argentinian working classes.

The Black Myth cites instances of sentiment on which, it claims, popular Peronism based its versions of the myth of Eva Perón. The evidence comes from records of Congressional or Cabinet sessions, the press of the régime, or the official school textbooks issued by the Peronist government. Anti-Peronists may have made the common mistake of confusing a political régime and its followers. But the fact remains that they have willingly believed evidence that consisted of exaggerated cases. They drew and still draw their conclusions about an entire social sector from sources which did not belong to it. To confirm the idea of a mystic cult of Eva Perón in the Peronist working classes, the anti-Peronists have used data which concerned the 'masses' but which the middle classes within Peronism generated.[65]

The Peronist middle class myth of the myth, many of the elements of which appeared in Peronist propaganda, may have given rise to the anti-Peronist version of the same belief. But chronological order is not of importance here: one version could inspire the other only because the groups that held both, though politically opposed, were united in the values that rendered them susceptible to the idea of a popular cult of Eva Perón. Why were both groups predisposed to believe so firmly in a popular cult of Eva Perón that, instead of developing the idea on the basis of evidence, they organized and interpreted facts according to this idea? Martínez Estrada, apologist for anti-Peronism, seemed to speak for orthodox Peronism as well when he based his conviction of the existence of such a cult on the fact that 'all the unformed and diffuse sentiments of a superstitition which needed an idol grounded their electrical charge through the death of the Spiritual Chief'.[66] The concept of a naturally superstitious or mystical Peronist following is one of the forms taken by another idea of the working classes which is widespread in the rest of Argentinian society. According to this common notion, the popular masses are composed of irrational beings who depend upon their emotions or instincts, or upon someone who appeals to these emotions and instincts, for their direction.

Anti-Peronists, when not attributing this irrationality to intrinsic mental, physical, or moral inferiority of individuals, groups, or races, blame it upon the corruption of the masses by demagogy or upon the debasing effects of membership in a mass according to theories of Freud.[67]

The negative value they place on every term of their formulation sometimes disguises it as a contradiction of any possible Peronist view. However, when the value sign for each element changes from negative to positive, the definition of the masses according to anti-Peronism reveals itself as basically the same. In the orthodox Peronist view, the people, because of intrinsically superior mental and moral traits, rely on their emotion and intuition which rightly lead them to devote themselves to a person, rather than to commit themselves with cold rationality to a set of causes.[68]

Anti-Peronism, like the ideology of groups that had opposed popular parties or popular elements in governments or parties before, yielded a wealth of imagery that carries the concept of the irrational masses to what seem to be its ultimate implications in the context of Argentinian culture. In order more clearly to suggest relationships that these ideas seem to exhibit with Eva Perón, the next chapter will investigate Argentinians' definitions of the popular sectors of their society

6

The Masses

Echoing imagery associated with a stereotype of womanhood, Argentinians have damned Eva Perón. Such condemnation exhibits a certain logic, as the previous analysis of the Peronist and anti-Peronist myths has suggested. Similar imagery appears in descriptions and definitions of the followers of this woman: the anti-Peronist image of the Peronist masses coincides with many of the negative elements used to discredit Eva Perón. This does not mean that Argentinians consider women natural leaders for the masses, nor is there any indication that they see the masses themselves as feminine. Rather a similar imagery defines both women and the masses as marginal to society's structures and values. Key to the configuration of negative elements used to describe the Peronist First Lady and the masses, thought to be her special followers, are concepts of their irrational natures, of the dominance in their lives of physical drives and instincts, and of their lack of culture and consequent approximation to a primitive state.

The negative image of the masses in Argentina has a long history. Similar criticism has arisen at different periods in different sectors to vilify equally different groups identified as mass movements. But despite the disparities in their contexts, sources, and objects, the descriptions display basic similarities. This chapter traces the resulting images through the three periods in Argentine history brought into focus earlier: the rule of Juan Manuel de Rosas in the mid-nineteenth century; the rise of Radicalism to power at the turn of the century; and the first Peronist régimes in the mid-twentieth century.

As this study has previously demonstrated, the element of emotional irrationality emerges not only in anti-Peronist images but also in Peronist thought, where it receives significant emphasis and positive value. Similar values underlie both Peronist propaganda and anti-Peronist opinion, and their similar emphases on the idea of the unreasoning, superstitious, and childishly emotional masses may imply further unstated similarities between them. Interviews eliciting comments about the party's mass following in a non-political context increase the impression that more negative elements are in fact shared with anti-Peronism by certain sectors of Peronism. Nevertheless, Peronist propaganda does not elaborate its image of the masses along all the lines of the anti-Peronist pattern of criticism. It is likely that the sectors of Peronism responsible for this literature only dared concentrate on the elements to which they could give positive value, such as, for example, notions about the intuitive masses. Other values associated with physical drives, especially sexuality, and primitivism are too strongly negative to be transformed.

The Argentinians themselves do not at present perceive a parallel between the mass followings of Radicalism and Peronism because the Radical party originally actually opposed the Peronists, forming part of the anti-Peronist coalition. In the process of incorporating the Radical Party into an anti-Peronist, anti-popular current of thought, some former enemies of the party came to see Radicalism and sometimes its leader Yrigoyen as repositories of those values which they had earlier accused them of negating.[1]

This chapter will describe the anti-Peronist, anti-Rosist, and anti-Radical images of the Argentinian masses in three sections organized around the central concepts that are also characteristic of criticism of Eva: irrationality, subjection to physical nature, and primitivism. Each group has attributed these traits to the popular following of its opponents, as well as to the leader of this following—the traits are associated with the images of Rosas and Yrigoyen as well as with the images of Eva. Each section will close with an indication of the perception and use by the Argentinians themselves of the parallels among the popular supporters of the three different régimes.

IRRATIONAL NATURE

The anti-Peronists who generated and believed the Black Myth and the Peronists who created and accepted the Lady of Hope both have held the concept of superstitious masses worshipping the image of Evita. The accusations and fears of the anti-Peronists concerning popular idolatry of the new 'Madre María' of the masses formed the counterpart of the laudatory and encouraging terms used by the Peronist press in its version of the enthusiasm of the masses for their 'Spiritual Chief'. Both images sprang from the conviction that the popular sectors of society actually worship their leaders. This belief bases itself in both versions on the idea that the common people are irrationally motivated, guided only by instinct and emotion. Of these ideas, neither the mystical nature of popular sentiments towards leaders nor the nature of the lower classes themselves are unique to the Peronist era and the following years. They also were important weapons in the arsenal of ideas used against both Rosas and Yrigoyen.

'The soul of the rabble [*populacho*]' appeared in the minds of the enemies of Rosas as prey to 'epidemic mysticism'. Characteristic superstition and religious fanaticism turned the mass following of the régime towards idolatrous worship of their leaders. When Rosas appeared on the scene, this pagan tendency drove the masses, in an extreme frenzy of enthusiasm, to deify the dictator. In these terms, Rosas' opponents referred to a custom of his régime that scandalized them all: placing portraits of the ruler in the churches of Buenos Aires.[2] Some claimed that the excited populace had placed the portrait of Rosas on the altar itself; others described the loyal crowds participating in religious processions that conducted the portrait through the streets, venerating it.[3]

Enemies of the Radical Party in the years of its early importance also feared what they saw as a populace focusing innate mystical tendencies on the adored figure of its leader. The opposition mixed criticisms of the Yrigoyenist masses with denunciations of the élite responsible for Radical propaganda directed at the people. Amongst both Conservatives and Socialists, many apparently did not doubt that the popular following of Yrigoyen adhered to the ideas which these same critics attributed to the Radical leadership. As in the case of Rosas, foes of Yrigoyen's leadership insisted that the masses actually rendered cult to their *caudillo* or to his image.

Opponents of Radicalism complained that the Radicals were not 'Regenerators', as they sometimes styled themselves, but 'mystifiers'. Yrigoyen had gained his popular support because he showed 'a predilection for shadows and . . . therefore certain rabble [*populacho*], which are so inclined towards obscurantism have believed that they see in this individual a new "hero of the holy cause of regeneration".'[4] The party succeeded amongst the masses by making

> its vague aspirations concrete in words, to the point that it constructed an entire oral and written mythology. And, in effect, all those senseless words . . . emitted an intention at once sentimental, epic, and even religious. They characterized a certain type of political obscurantism; something of masonry with something of a secret society [*carbonarismo*].[5]

The population responded to these official overtures, according to the opposition, with a mystical emotion expressed in the vocabulary of formal religion. Anti-Radicalists shuddered at the thought that the fervour of Yrigoyen's followers had caused them to issue stamps in his honour, some of which took a specifically religious form in the northern provinces of Argentina, areas where both poverty and Indian influence were believed to be widespread. In similar regions, hostile accounts held, the poor lit candles before the portrait of Yrigoyen. The idea of this kind of behaviour earned for Yrigoyenism the epithet of 'magical radicalism'.[6]

The parallels amongst these versions did not escape their creators. On the contrary, the parallels themselves contributed importantly to the negative image of the different political figures.

Stories concerning the apparently purely secular cases of commemorative or even postal stamps honouring the Radicals took on connotations of heathen religion when related to other cases from the time of Rosas, which were specifically linked with religious practices. In some works the examples from the Rosas régime exhibit little relation to those from the Radical years, except in their proximity on the same or adjacent pages, but such juxtaposition tends to equate Radical commemorative stamps with the placing of the portrait of Rosas on the altar of the churches of Buenos Aires. Similarly, the issuance of Radical postal stamps is likened in motivation to the processions that carried the portrait of Rosas through the streets of the capital, while a parallel is established between the vague memory of religious stamps and candles dedicated to Yrigoyen amongst the poor in distant provinces and the alleged worship of Rosas in the churches of the capital city.[7]

The same rhetorical devices were used to show that party colours, devices, and so forth under Yrigoyen resembled the symbols and practices of the Rosas régime, 'an era during which symbolism, which has many elements of ceremonious religiosity and ritualism, was adopted and respected by all classes'. It was pointed out as proof of the existence of such religious and ritualistic symbolism that 'Rosas made obligatory the use of bright red'.[8]

Still other versions confirmed their conclusions about the evil of Rosas or Yrigoyen by comparing one with the other and concluding that both formed the centres of 'myths' or 'mystery'. When Perón appeared, his enemies termed his appeal to the masses as mystical and made the derogatory note in such a label unmistakable in comparisons of all three régimes: Rosist, Radical, and Peronist.[9]

PHYSIOLOGICAL DRIVES: SEX AND VIOLENCE

The anti-Peronist mind connects the mysticism and irrationality of followers of Peronism with domination by their own physical nature. All-invading lust and inborn violence rule the lives of the men and women of mass Peronism. Their uncontrolled sexuality transformed the Peronist government into a ' "pornocracy" ' whose 'official acts, ceremonies, and Saturnalia . . . revived ancient processional phallic cults diguised by the emblems of the fatherland and liberty'.[10]

The combination of physiological instincts with an unreflecting mysticism emerged in one of its most extreme—and, for the anti-Peronist, most disgusting—forms in the scandalous events after the death of the Spiritual Chief of the Nation. Bereaved Peronists formed their endless line down the streets of the city centre awaiting a chance to pay their respects to the body, which enemies predicted would become the central relic of a pagan cult. In a short story describing the days of mourning, an anti-Peronist approaches the line, where he fully expects to encounter an easy sexual conquest. With no trouble he finds a willing mourner. They leave the vigil on a frenzied search for a hotel room, only to find the hotels closed in honour of the deceased Eva. Only at this point, when the anti-Peronist carelessly insults the dead idol of his companion, does she angrily rebuff him, leaving him frustrated and bewildered.[11]

Characteristic outbursts of animal nature, as conceived by the anti-Peronist, also occur outside the context of mysticism. In his campaign speeches, Enrique Mosca, vice-presidential candidate of those who opposed Perón in 1945, spoke of 'indecent and noisy groups which move us to pity'. Although he did not define the terms in detail, his repeated use of such expressions as 'the primary passions' and the 'lower appetites' indicate that he associated—and expected his audiences to associate—sexual and physical drives with the popular following of Juan Perón.[12]

The anti-Peronist press revealed a similar association when it reported a chant which it attributed to Peronist women: 'Without shirts and without pants/We are all for Perón [*Sin camisa y sin calzón/Todas somos de Perón*]!'[13] Argentinian informants react to this rhyme with no surprise or shock and may go on to chant similar jingles used at games in their schools. They see in it only harmless and humorous sexual implications or none at all. However, the news report declared that the chant caused problems between Eva Perón and other female Peronists because the words incited the First Lady's jealousy. Thus the press assumed, or hoped that its readers would assume, that the lines were to be taken literally and as an indication of the type of attraction that Perón exercised over his female followers.

Anti-Peronism in both contemporary interview and literature from the Peronist decade has attributed to the Argentinian masses a violence as basic to their nature as their diffused sexuality. Anti-Peronists today, who describe the vast groups of Argentinian slum dwellers as naturally alcoholic and violent, repeat unawares the ideas of Mosca in 1945, when he spoke of 'the savage outbreaks of the illiterate hordes stupefied by alcohol'. The press depicted the provinces under Peronist popular governments degenerating into something resembling a general free-for-all in which knifings to the cry of 'Viva Perón!' were common, whether in the country bars or in the houses of government.[14]

Mosca's speeches went further in linking the idea of the violence of the lower strata of society with their sexuality.[15] This association is elaborated in another short story, in which a lone anti-Peronist encounters a group of Peronists on the street. The gang threatens him with violence if he refuses to shout 'Viva Perón!' Simultaneously, one of them makes homosexual overtures to him. The band then falls into a crudely sexual dance around a woman who egged them on in their assault on the defenceless pedestrian.

> The dance continued: it was something brutal and attractive; all of them mixed, shoving each other rudely, loosely, with their clothing hanging as though it bothered them and they were about to rip it off or as though they were wishing that it would slide off them onto the ground.[16]

Throughout the rest of the tale, the victim evokes with dread the phantom of the Peronist masses, symbolized by the dancing woman with her 'shamelessly low neckline'.

Anti-Rosists anticipated by a century anti-Peronist ideas of a hated popular régime and its leaders. A description of festive occasions under Rosas as 'banquets and balls . . . a type of Bacchanal, true orgies' prefigured the anti-Peronist definition of the occasion at which Perón and Eva Duarte first met: 'It was a dance, a party, a Bacchanal'.[17] Similarly, parallels to anti-Peronist ideas about the fascination exercised over the masses by a popular leader appeared in accounts of the relation of Rosas to his following:

> The women of the plebe loved [*amaban*] Rosas in an almost animal form . . . More animal in fact because their adhesion and admiration had the same exuberance as the mating urge, and their brief popular encounters, the proportions of copulation. . . . Backward in all intellectual activities, the black woman lived only for the heat of her diverse forms of physical admiration, of personal loyalty, of almost animal adhesion.[18]

These extreme affirmations distort other anti-Rosist reports[19] to which they refer but which contain no suggestion of the animal sexuality emphasized here. But the press at that time, in attempts to discredit Rosas' wife and other Federalist matrons, printed scurrilous accounts of their illicit love-making. The use of sexual imagery for purposes of propaganda already existed in the Rosas and post-Rosas ambience.

Rosas' violence almost overwhelms all other themes in common denunciations of his years in power. The opponents, past and present, of Federalism immediately associate the name of Rosas with The

Terror as well as with two of the most important tools of its implemen-
tation, the Mazorca and the Sociedad Popular Restauradora.
Perhaps the maximum expression of the association of violence with
the masses, the *'chusma'*, of the time continues to form a part of the
education of many Argentinians when they read Esteban Echeverría's
classic, *'El matadero'*, 'The Slaughterhouse'. In the tale, uneducated
butchers torture and kill an aristocratic youth in the middle of the
blood and violence of the slaughterhouse, described as the focus of
Rosas' régime.[20]

Both elements—the sexual and the violent—of the 'almost totally
physiological drive' of the 'popular mass'[21] reappeared in the propaganda directed against the Radical Party. Criticism aimed against
the Radical régimes repeated suggestions of links with sexuality and
also concentrated upon violence.

Different versions established similar associations between Radicalism and sex. The Radical party owed its success to an 'erotic mysticism' typical of Argentinian mass culture, demonstrated in this case
by posters proclaiming 'Yrigoyen in the heart of the people'. At the
same time, the corruption of the régime derived ultimately from the
moral state of its leader, who 'was not born or brought up in the
warm glow of familial honour and has accustomed his eyes to see
immorality under his roof'. Meanwhile, pornography proliferated,
due not precisely to the Radical movement itself, but to the common
causes of Radicalism and 'the excesses of liberty committed in the era':

> Every period of demagogy (do not forget that demagogy, govern-
> ment of the multitudes which has arisen as the effect of a crisis . . . is
> the sign of a distortion of the moral senses) . . . is characterized by the
> exaltations, glorification of delinquency, etc. . . . Pornographic litera-
> ture takes form.[22]

Argentinians today still recall the wide diffusion of tales of violence
under Yrigoyen. They remember rumours of thugs who surrounded
the ex-President and committed outrages at his instigation. In-
criminations of the notorious Radical Clan as a far-reaching and
much-feared system of organized crime depict it as a necessary concomitant of Radicalism, usually omitting the fact that it operated
only during Yrigoyen's last year in power. A contemporary denunci-
ation of the Radical régime diagnosed, 'It is the initiation of system-
atized terror; it is collective assassination which is being cast over

the people to oppress them by means of fear'. This version echoed Echeverría's description of the slaughterhouse, and foreshadowed anti-Peronism's fear of Peronist-instigated chaos, claiming that 'the fist fight is the desideratum of democracy of the slums', and that this form of dispute was replacing rational deliberation in the government itself.[23]

Enemies of the Radical Party and of Yrigoyen himself associated both with the violence of the *arrabal*, the distinctive culture of the outskirts of Buenos Aires, far more than they did Conservative groups or politicians. Yrigoyen dominated the Argentinian masses as the 'last caudillo', skilfully manipulating 'creole politics'.[24]

Again, both in conversation and literature, Argentinian political criticism exploits parallels amongst descriptions of different groups and their leaders. One account may be concerned to establish the existence of a blossoming pornography not only under Yrigoyen but also under Rosas, while another may affirm that all dictatorships in Argentina depend on 'erotic mysticism'.[25] Both anti-Radical and anti-Peronist literature frequently link the violence of the régimes they condemn with that of the Rosist era.[26] Sometimes a mere repetition of incidents or ideas linked with the terror of Rosas is sufficient. In this way they attempt to transfer the aspersion involved from one figure to another; quoting at length, for example, from Sarmiento's denunciations of the Rosas era in *Facundo* to imply unqualified application of his descriptions to the Peronist case. Similarly, ' "the climate of 'El matadero' " ' becomes the equivalent of ' "the social and political moment of the Perón years" ' while Peronism becomes 'violent bands which appear on the scene of our struggle to relive the fatal deeds of the era of the *mazorca*'.[27]

LÈSE-CIVILIZATION

Popular anti-Peronist opinion holds one of the greatest deficiencies of the Peronist masses to be their lack of culture. Argentinians refer to culture as a category containing not only education, but, perhaps even more importantly, refinement in manners and taste. Accusations of the lack of this vague attribute take widely varied forms. Anti-Peronists re-tell in shocked tones the story of the original sultry October 17, when the Peronist crowds took off their shoes and waded in the ornamental fountains of the Plaza de Mayo. Or they may go further, applying epithets such as the 'zoological alluvion' to Peronists. The different versions taken together reproach the masses more emphatically for their lack of 'good taste' and their failure to adhere to certain rules of etiquette and comportment than for their scant academic education or intellectual and artistic cultivation.[28] Anti-Peronism pits civilization in general against chaos, primitivism, and even animality—incarnate in mass Peronism.

Anti-Peronists reveal their emphasis on taste in a wealth of commentary in which they denigrate the dress of the Peronist élite. Some groups directed a certain amount of censure against an ideological contradiction implied by this elegance.[29] But anti-Peronists stress their enemies' lack of sartorial taste and the bearing necessary to choose and wear the supposedly unaccustomed garments. The Peronists failed in their attempts at dressing themselves in a way appropriate to the position in society which they now felt was theirs. The Minister of Labour, Freire, a former worker, appeared in an anti-Peronist caricature dressed in a tuxedo which, the text claimed, came from one of the most aristocratic tailors of Buenos Aires. Yet the figure of Freire slumped on the page, was sloppily garbed, unshaven, and had a large cigar protruding from his mouth. It was said that the patent leather dress shoes which the new ruling class had donned began to pinch their exaggeratedly wide feet. When a group of union representatives lunched with Eva Perón in their shirtsleeves, their customary symbolic statement of their identity as 'shirtless ones', an anti-Peronist report of the event proclaimed them 'Not descamisados; boors [*guarangos*]'.[30]

Anti-Peronism, in waging its first campaign against Perón and his followers, availed itself frequently of the symbolism of Peronism's violation of 'the majesty of culture' in all its forms. Mosca constantly damned his enemies by identifying them with a negation of culture and civilization, terms which he makes synonymous, hurling jibes that range from 'illiterate hordes' through 'low morality [*bajeza moral*]' to 'primitivism', 'savagery', and repeated charges of barbarism.[31]

The enemies of Rosas wielded the idea of his followers' lack of culture against them in similar ways. They disparaged Rosas' popular supporters for their low intellectual level; for their poor taste, and worse, their attempts to imitate the taste and mien of their social superiors; for their primitive traits that betrayed recent development from, or close association with, the savage state that supposedly still reigned in the Argentinian interior. These opponents often intended direct complaints about the support of the government and the participation in it of the vast sectors of the Argentinian population which had had little or no contact with formal education. In this sense, 'in order to be Governor, the most respectable degree was that of knowing how to ride horseback well, being a bronco buster'.[32] Under such a régime 'even the language which had been spoken before had been perverted; new words circulated: rough, acrid, unused'.[33] Implications of this were wide at the time:

> To follow a people in its phonetic transformations is to decipher little by little the mystery of its soul, its psychological rhythm.

> The savages do not have history, their language being as poor as their means of subsistence and well-being. Usually they do not even have either tradition or memory; their existence, in this sense, is not human, it is a biological state; animality [*animalidad*] . . .

> Consequently, if a higher or lower degree of civilization implies greater or lesser lack of material culture [*carencia de las cosas*], it also implies plethora or paucity of symbols [*signos representativos*]; and the increasing or decreasing use of these necessarily constitutes ascending or descending grades of culture.[34]

Anti-Rosists distinguished between Rosists who, pretentiously and unsuccessfully, imitated European culture and standards and those who completely lacked both. The faults represented very different social sectors: the *guarangos*, 'the bridge between the plebe and the patricians, as the mollusc is between the invertebrates and those who already have a skeleton'; and the 'huge and ignorant gauchos'.[35]

The '*guarangocracia*' lived to imitate and hate the 'patricians' and their supposedly unimpeachable European culture. According to anti-Rosist opinion, 'guarangos' staunchly supported Rosas, while true aristocrats espoused the cause of the opposition. Social molluscs inevitably failed in their imitation of the patricians because they suffered from an innate and irremediable cultural inferiority, which revealed itself in their 'aesthetic sense, still grotesque'. Such a judgement permeates an Argentinian classic of the time, José Mármol's *Amalia*, while the distinction it implies re-emerged almost a century later to differentiate between the distinguished culture of the original Federalists and the lack of any such quality on the part of the followers of Rosas in the later schism in the movement.[36]

Rosas' enemies saw the plebeian element of Federalism as a horde of gauchos, blacks, and mulattos, ready to overwhelm the 'civilization' of the cosmopolitan city of Buenos Aires. The opposition used concepts of the inherent inferiority of mestizo and black blood as darts aimed at so unlikely a target as the golden-haired Rosas himself. Unitarians called him 'mulatto' in reference 'not ... to his colour (he was so blond!), but rather to his deeds': popular prejudice held that the mulatto was particularly untrustworthy. This idea found so ready an acceptance in the general anti-Rosist public that it was taken literally: when the handsome, blond ruler rode by, onlookers who believed that Rosas had dark skin sometimes anxiously asked who had passed in the midst of such clamour.[37] Rosas' followers were believed to be dark skinned and apparently concomitantly, primitive and animal: 'hairy and simian, complexion grotesque and toasted, eyes ferocious'. 'Barbarious and dark ... bloody and semi-savage', these beings threatened to dominate their rational and civilized opponents by brute force. When they governed, Argentina was subjected to rule by the 'hungry and shirtless': '[los] *hambrientos y descamisados*'.[38]

The adversaries of Yrigoyen and the Radicals claimed that they attempted vainly to attain culture or totally lacked all vestiges of it or any motivation to attain it. 'He who attends a theatre ... will be able to classify as Radical all who are badly dressed and have long hair or who behave themselves in a gross manner or with excessive humility.' As the antithesis of culture, Hipólito Yrigoyen shut out 'any manifestation of science or art': 'They instil in him an uneasiness and distrust which he cannot overcome. They are creatures of Europe; European culture annoys him. It is the unknown, the enemy'.[39]

Anti-Radicalism did not define the concepts of culture and civilization any more than did the opponents of the Rosas or Perón régimes. Nevertheless, it also provides a wealth of associated ideas, with implications similar to those uncovered in the two cases just examined. Anti-Radicals discerned a type of intellectual formation and artistic appreciation; comportment which testified to 'distinction' and 'good taste'; and 'details of luxury and aesthetics ... delicate and noble epicureanisms which fuse themselves with beauty and art'. The enemies of Radical power, then, included aesthetic values in their political judgements on grounds such as the idea of 'Beauty and Art as the foundation of morality, religion and the force of nations'.[40]

The opposition qualified the general atmosphere under Radicalism as 'semi-literate', ridiculing the common assumption of the title of 'Doctor' by any Radical, and especially by Yrigoyen himself.[41] The enemies of Yrigoyenism became even more obsessed with the disintegration of language under its influence than did the enemies of Federalism. They protested grammatical and phonetic deformations, which they saw as related to ideological distortions and inferior states of civilization. All of this they associated in turn with the creole and the immigrant. The nation found itself in terrible straits, where 'all the vices . . . separate us from correct syntax, and the prepositional régime suffers as much as the institutional régime'.[42]

Anti-Yrigoyenists, like anti-Rosists and anti-Peronists, derided the failures of the Radicals in their efforts to appropriate the outward appearances of a social status higher than their own. A similar pre-occupation with lack of taste and bearing necessary to assume certain dress and mannerisms gave rise to insults revealing the anti-Peronist and Peronist struggle to be less original than it might otherwise have seemed. Opponents of Radicalism scornfully emphasized that, when Yrigoyen made his triumphal entry into the Government Palace, 'narrow shoes tortured his feet'. A few hours after the new President had assumed office, a scion of one of the prominent families of the aristocracy exclaimed, 'It has been terrible . . . We have passed from the dress slipper to the work shoe—to the *alpargata*!'[43]

This emphasis on refinement of taste and mien transforms the *compadrito*, key figure in the power structure and violence that under-lay the political system of *comités* of the period, into a dandy distin-guished by his exaggerated imitation of the elegant upper classes of Buenos Aires. As described at the time, the *compadrito*, degenerated from the gaucho, grotesquely and futilely attempted to reach the always undefined but highly desirable state of the man of culture, '*hombre culto*'. One word summed up the latest and worst form assumed by the *compadrito*: he was *guarango*.[44]

Exalting culture as a specifically European phenomenon, Argen-tinians defined a lack of it as a primitive state, consisting of retro-gression, delinquency, and amorality. Both the Conservative *caudillos* and the popular following of Radicalism were accused often by each other—of primitivism. The rather sober middle-class image of the Radical Party today, promoted by itself and by the different régimes since the Peronist decade, belies the idea that its opponents could ever have considered the social sectors it represents atavistic in any way, still less that they could have described the Radicals in terms such as 'bloody', 'barbarous', and 'almost aboriginal'. Yet the Radicals appeared to their opponents as primitivism incarnate, as the 'hordes' of *barbarie*, which supposedly threatened art, science, and civilization itself.[45]

Their enemies saw these hordes as 'impulsive and capricious', a force of nature like any other. The mental operations of the Yrigoyenists were limited to instinct, 'magic and shamanism [*curanderismo*]', 'awkward emotionalism [*sentimentalismo*] and nebulous ideology of the primitives'. Identifications of Radicalism with the creole soul, with indigenous blood, or with the mestizo and gaucho sometimes gave explicit statement to racism only implicit elsewhere:[46] *¡ Helas! Somos también South America* [sic]! . . . The fatal inheritance, converted into a species . . . bites us from behind, treacherously . . . ! Such is . . . this shameful crime of lèse-republic and of lèse-civilisation.[47]

During the Radical governments, the opposition took advantage of the resemblances they perceived between the uncultured state of the crowds that followed both Yrigoyen and Rosas. While some objected to the similar degeneration of language, others constructed a sort of genealogy to connect the Radical *guarango* or Yrigoyenist with the gaucho or even the Indian.[48] The similar comparison of the Peronists with the societies of blacks under Rosas and their African religious ceremonies or *candombe* dances testified to the supposed similar cultural level of the two groups. An undocumented quote from Sarmiento diagnosed the situation under Perón, stating, 'The brute Juan Manuel would not have been an idol if there had not been so many brutes in the country'. (The word 'brute [*bruto*]' in Argentinian Spanish connotes, perhaps even more than animal nature, a stupidity aggravated by a lack of refinement and education.) Another comparison amongst the eras, drawing in Radicalism as well, presented as equivalents the closing of the university and the expulsion of the Jesuits under Rosas with the pretentious use of the title 'Doctor' by Yrigoyen and the slogan *'Alpargatas sí, libros no'* [Workshoes yes, books no] of Peronism.[49]

In sum, anti-Rosists, anti-Radicals, and anti-Peronists criticized the mass followings of their enemies in similar terms. But this portrayal of the masses represents more than a formal resemblance based on the comparison of documents from different eras. Argentinians themselves have drawn the parallels involved and have referred to them in the literature examined here as well as in current conversations; they are able to adduce them and manipulate their historical associations as negatively valued symbols.

But the analogies established in this way do not arise for the most part from actual similarities amongst groups, régimes, and eras. The sociological, political, and historical differences amongst the cases involved preclude the possibility of drawing valid parallels on the lines suggested by the patterns of criticism. The currents of opinion drew similarities from highly disparate contexts.

Eva Perón may have coincided with this pattern as a whole or provided a convenient screen onto which it could be projected. This may account for the fact that she became a focal point of hatred and a prime reason in herself for her enemies' rejection of the politics that she represented. The opposition has rejected in Eva Perón more than a political stand: they repudiate the threat of dominance of a group believed to negate culture and society, their forms, rules, hierarchies, and values as the anti-Peronists knew them.

7
Eva The Revolutionary

¡Si Evita viviera/sería montonera!
If Evita lived/she would fight with the guerrilla!

—Slogan and street chant, 1972

The mythology surrounding Eva Perón contains imagery explicitly associated with a feminine ideal, uncontrolled power, and revolutionary leadership. The links postulated have appeared in two images of Eva Perón that form essentially two versions of the same myth, arising from the same social sector but from adherents of different political beliefs. But a different myth of Eva Perón exists in Argentina, offering further proof of these symbolic connections. It can only be understood in the light of these connections as they appear in the myths already discussed.

To Peronists of the Left, Eva Perón has personified not the affirmation or negation of a feminine ideal, but revolutionary Peronism itself. Myths of the revolutionary Eva do not express her radical role in terms of a feminine ideal. Theirs is a much more historical and circumstantial account of her special type of revolutionary leadership. But they do use terms similar to those that describe her power in both Peronist and anti-Peronist myths. All three versions associate an uninstitutionalized power with emotion, intuition, disorder. All three versions link these traits with a woman and with the masses. And all contrast the spiritual sway the woman exercises by virtue of these traits with the institutionalized office, legitimate authority, and rational leadership which they attribute to a man, Juan Perón.

EVA PERÓN: REVOLUTIONARY

The guerrilla forces of the Left have called on Eva—not Juan—
Perón as the inspiration of their spirit and commitment to battle:

> When we are discouraged, we draw our strength from Eva Perón. She
> is the example of the revolution; she is the revolutionary spirit. She
> exemplified personal force at the service of the revolution: the dedi-
> cation to the process of change, to the accomplishment of a goal. In all
> this she is like *el che* Guevara. For us Evita is the spirit of the guerrilla.
> Juan Perón is the content of the resistance: we fight in order to bring
> back Perón, and we fight with many of his tactics. But we are fighting
> because of Evita—and for her.[1]

To many Peronists, Eva, the woman herself, was the revolutionary
element within their movement: Eva Perón as a person acted in a
way that no one else dared act. She disregarded rules, disobeyed
protocol, broke traditions with an impunity no one else was permitted.
She began projects, fanned emotions, defended ideas with an originality of which no one else was capable. The role she created for
herself became, as it developed, an option within Peronism: at first a
possible mode of action and, later, with the action, a revolutionary
concept based on it.

Followers of the militant Eva who describe her importance to
themselves and to their movement allow the relation of events and
their analysis to overlap as they do, accordingly, in these pages. Informants themselves made the explanations, analyses, and commentary presented here, with the exceptions of the chapter conclusions
and the mention of Eva's arms purchase. For these Peronists, a
separation between Eva's life story and its ideological significance
was impossible.

In explaining the revolutionary image of Eva Perón to outsiders,
many Peronists first qualify it in order to avoid the notorious errors
of interpretation often found amongst both Peronists and anti-
Peronists.

They protest any translation of Evita's stand into Marxist terms.
Peronism has included Marxist thought and elements, and some
within the movement have claimed Eva's position to be the 'most
clearly classist in the nation' at her time.[2] But much of the rest of
Peronism repudiates this opinion, accepting Marxist ideas only when
applied to, and duly modified by, Argentinian Peronist experience.

Peronists who see the relevance of Marxism in this way qualify Peronist Marxist ideas in that they consider those who hold them neither truly Argentinian nor of working class origin, and only recently incorporated into the party. Peronists deduce this from the association of Marxism in Argentinian history and society with anti-Peronism—in particular, with immigrant European workers and groups of middle and upper class students and intellectuals, all of whom were vociferously hostile during Perón's régime. In years before the return of Perón to Argentina, the Argentine Marxist Left drew closer to Peronism. But Peronists still often feel that their movement's Marxist members and some of the elements of theory they have introduced do not take into full account either the historical and cultural tradition that Peronists consider truly Argentinian and uniquely theirs, or the years of formative experience in early Peronism and in the later Resistance to the subsequent anti-Peronist governments.

In answer to claims of class-consciousness for Eva Perón, large numbers of Peronists today emphasize what they see as one of the basic ideas of their current ideology as it has developed and been clarified over the past twenty-seven years of growth: The Peronist movement, according to many of its members and theorists today, is most importantly an anti-imperialistic movement and therefore is not representative of one class only, but of many. For those who adhere to this formulation of Peronist ideology, Eva did not promote a 'clearly classist' revolution. In this view, her actions proclaimed, in one of its first and truest statements, the opposition of oppressors and oppressed. She based her position not on theory but on experience and unerring intuition. But now, say the Peronists who share this position, that position has come to be recognized as a characteristic of developing nations of colonial origin and thus as an important element of the reality of the entire Third World. Her followers most often detect this idea in Eva's statements in the form of her defence of her 'shirtless ones' against the 'oligarchy'.

Some Peronists interpret Eva's accusations against the 'oligarchs' within her own movement to imply a recognition on her part that those who did not actively further revolutionary Peronism, by virtue of this fact alone, allied themselves with an opposite force. This force acted not only against Peronism but, more importantly, in favour of international capitalism and its imperialistic economy in which, still according to this version of Eva's ideas, significant sectors of Argentinian society collaborate.

Those who affirm that Eva's was no 'classist' or strictly Marxist position often support this idea by their interpretation of the two books attributed to Eva Perón in which, they emphasize, she stressed 'spirit' over origin as the defining elements in the Argentinian social conflict:

> For me, therefore, *a shirtless one* is he who feels himself part of the people. That is what is important . . . although he may not dress like the humble people, something which is incidental.[3]

> I know that the oligarchy, the oligarchy of October 12, 1945 which gathered in the Plaza San Martín, will not return to government, but that is not the oligarchy whose return worries me. What worries me is that the oligarchic spirit might return in us . . . and in order that this does not occur I must struggle . . . so that no one lets himself be tempted by vanity, by privilege, by pomp, and by ambition.[4]

EVA AND JUAN

The revolutionary Eva created an essential part of Peronism. Yet Perón claimed to have created Eva. Peronists accept this claim, but simultaneously they feel that Perón in the early years of Peronism was himself incapable of Eva's insights and innovations. In the myth of a militant Eva, followers of the two leaders resolve this paradox through an account of the histories and characters of Juan and Eva and of their relations with each other.

In this version Colonel Juan Perón already possessed a growing reputation as a brilliant military strategist and increasingly skilful politician when he met Evita Duarte. His life and specific training from the time of his adolescence in a military academy equipped him to participate in traditional power spheres. He knew how to negotiate and bargain with other sectors of society and their interests in their conventional terms. This capacity he had begun to employ in the defence of the working classes. Perón showed a great intellectual understanding of the problems of the Argentinian masses, and commanded the theoretical knowledge and strategic talent necessary to further the cause of the people.

But Peronists affirm that, although Perón himself came from a humble family, his life had not given him the total identification with Argentina's poorer classes and the empathy with their problems that Eva Duarte demonstrated. His followers often state that in the early years of his relationship with Evita, Perón still basically identified himself with military modes of action, although he already differed with the basic goals of the armed forces. At this early period in his political and personal development, he still could not share Eva's complete disregard of established traditions, forms, and rules.

In Eva Duarte, this version continues, Juan Perón encountered a young woman who still showed the marks of a constantly unstable, sometimes deeply tragic, childhood. Like Perón, she was an illegitimate child in a provincial family. Her personal misfortunes and those of the Argentinians who formed the lower strata of their society were perceived, first by Eva and later by these poorer classes, as similar. In this sense it is Eva, the aspiring actress, rather than Juan, the military cadet made good, who in her childhood, in her adolescent struggles, and in the vicissitudes of her career, suffered the economic frustration, political impotence and social humiliation of the Argentinian working class—and of the lowest of the low within that class, the scorned *cabecita negra* of the interior. Eva's earlier experiences heightened her innate social consciousness and convinced her of the widespread injustice of society in her country.

But these feelings and the conclusions the young Evita drew from them remained at first unarticulated and subordinated to her personal ambition. To Eva and to many in her position, unashamed ambition, in the form of sexual prostitution or brazen manipulation of others, represented the only key to an escape from the limitations of the existence to which less fortunate Argentinians were born. Many young women may have arrived in the capital from the interior with similar confusions of thoughts and emotions in their minds. At least, many Peronists think that this is probable. But they also feel that Evita Duarte was different: she was more intelligent than most; she possessed a deeper sensitivity than most; and it was she who met and chose, and was chosen by, Juan Domingo Perón.

Perón, with twice her years and experience, confirmed her intuitions, structured her insights and offered her a channel for her intelligence, sensitivity and energy. Without the catalytic effect of Perón in her life, Eva Duarte would have come to nothing. She would neither have understood nor participated in political action or power.

In this way, those who follow her as the revolutionary vanguard of Peronism can nevertheless state that Juan Perón created Eva Perón. From their meeting she was born.

Within weeks Eva Duarte was working for Perón's cause in the Secretariat of Labour and Welfare. Enthusiasts for Eva's revolutionary activism give Perón full credit for making room from the beginning in his life and his politics for the elements represented by Eva Duarte. He knew their value and recognized them as necessary: Peronists have confidence that, had Eva not lived, Perón would have found another person, institution, or strategy through which to incorporate these elements into Peronism. Peronists will say that Perón and Peronism would have been the same without María Eva Duarte de Perón. But without Juan Perón, Eva Perón would never have existed.

Yet both Juan Perón and Eva Duarte did exist; they did meet; they married; and together they created Peronism. Peronists hold that the process need not have occurred in this way, but it did. It was therefore not only a political process but a personal one as well.

The fact that she owed her position to Perón in no way diminished Eva in Peronist eyes. Her attitude, her talent and above all her intuition formed an essential basis of the political process on which they embarked together and of the role within it for which Perón prepared her. A Peronist militant denigrating Perón's third wife, Isabel Martínez, before her return to Argentina with Perón, quipped, 'There is, after all, a question of raw material. No matter how much anyone tries to prepare Isabelita, there is no result whatsoever'.[5]

And, too, Eva Perón's fidelity to Perón and Peronism did not limit her to obeying orders. Peronists assert that she expressed her loyalty rather in carrying her concept of Peronism to its last implications— implications that frequently, at the time, she alone understood. This interpretation holds that only in the last few years did many of Eva's actions and statements gradually become comprehensible to Peronists in general and incorporated by Perón into his official ideology. Many Peronists state that the terms in which Eva's life is now construed as an ideological stand would not have been understood by her followers during her lifetime. Eva Perón, the woman, was thus in many ways herself an ideological element which, though it existed within the movement, could not be integrated into Peronist politics of her time.

In the eyes of militant Peronists, if Eva consciously accepted the role for which Perón shaped her as well as the subordinate position it implied, she did so because she herself had come to understand her part. She wanted to and was able to play the role within the Peronist movement as conceived and conducted by Juan Perón. In this way she formed part of Perón, an identity she never betrayed. She never promoted herself or her image as independent of Perón, even on the grounds of her independent projects or power. And her first concern and last words were to exhort her followers to 'Take care of Perón'.

The image of the revolutionary Eva, then, implies a certain relationship between the apparently distinct orientations of the two leaders: the difference between Eva and Juan Perón did not reflect any basic disharmony, ideological or otherwise, but rather a simple division of labour. Juan Perón assumed the administrative, governmental activities of the party strategist, while Eva acted out and fiercely protected the most radical interpretations of Peronist ideology. Without contradicting Perón's cooperation and compromises with the very sectors which she rejected, Eva took on the contrasting role, characteristic of her, of the representation of the masses as well as the opposition to bureaucratic and other conservative elements within Peronism. Perón allowed Eva, under his leadership, to dominate in the areas in which her action was appropriate. In these areas she set precedents that could never be ignored and whose implications represented a particular ideological option within the movement.

Perón's role was necessary for the practical survival of the movement; Eva's role essential to its continued progress. Due to the political genius of Juan Perón, both positions were able to coexist in the party and Peronism could profit by both tactics.

Few Peronists, as they themselves emphasize, claim to have completely analysed and understood as a coherent formula either Peronist ideology or Peronist strategy. Eva, with her personal force and innovativeness, made a place in the movement for continuing questioning and change in a particular direction, just as Perón made a place for the ongoing strategic leadership in a particular style and towards a particular goal. In part, Eva's ideology and Juan's strategy can be analysed. But there remains another part of each for which the contradictory and original human beings, Eva and Juan, their personalities and the events each lived, are totally responsible.

Peronists, then, sometimes claim that Eva Perón *is* Peronist ideology in the same way that Juan Perón *is* Peronist strategy. Long before anyone elaborated analyses of Eva's role and labelled them as ideologies, revolutionary Peronism had intuitively imitated and invoked Eva Perón, the person she was and the militancy she lived, until she became the inspiration of the Peronist revolution.

While her relationship with Perón was still forming, followers of the militant Eva relate, the events of October 17, 1945 contributed significantly to the creation of Eva Perón as a revolutionary figure. The first mass demonstration in support of Perón marked this day as all-important in Peronist history. On that day, this version holds, Eva dedicated herself totally to the working masses of nascent Peronism; and on that day the conditions arose for the development of the forces within Peronism itself that would oppose her in her representation of the poor.

All Argentina remembers October 17 as the date the masses erupted into the country's political power spheres. A new kind of participation in political life in general was born. But some Peronists believe that an increasingly opportunistic bureaucracy also began on that day to corrupt the movement, gradually usurping the place of the masses.

Her followers express little interest in the exact role of the young mistress of Argentina's new popular leader in rescuing him from exile on October 17. Some claim that it was she who organized the vast demonstration of the workers of Buenos Aires who gathered before the Government House, leaving their factories and jobs a day before the recently set general strike, to demand the freedom of their hero, Perón. Some feel that she only participated, as they all did, anonymously in the streets, another of the thousands making their way to the Plaza de Mayo. On whatever level her participation took place, the significance of the day in her life remains the same in the context of her revolutionary image.

This experience formed the basic conviction, manifested through Eva Perón's later political career, of the power and purity of the active loyalty that a people can offer a leader. She and the jubilant crowds of that day discovered with new loyalties, a new manner of defending them, and with new goals, a new way of reaching them. They had discovered an anonymous yet aggressive mode of action, which was to identify an Evita and a mass following of Peronism which from that moment occupied positions in the forefront of their movement.

'She learned in this way', stated a spokesman for the Priests of the Third World, 'how a people, a Leader, and a faith are born and are made . . . She and those who accompanied her saved Perón and Peronism, but only because they bet on the combativity of the people, a combativity which in that moment seemed illusory and impossible.'[6] In different words, a Peronist factory worker made the same affirmation: 'The significance of October 17 for Evita lies in her decision and capacity to confide in her class, to deposit confidence in the working class. That was one of her greatest roles'.[7]

To the proponents of Peronist revolution, October 17 today symbolizes the weaknesses as well as the strengths inherent in Peronism at its birth. For them the revolution lasted one day only. They consider its success too facile, allowing the early bureaucratization of the movement, a negative facet they feel has marked the entire subsequent history of Peronism. When it dedicated its energies to participation in the very system it tried to change, Peronism was debilitated and even corrupted from the beginning. Revolutionary Peronism, often underground, accuses orthodox Peronists of allowing their inclusion in the electoral system to hamper their ideological development, in some senses, of stagnating completely.

The account of Eva as revolutionary goes on to say that these weaknesses, one practical and the other ideological, gave special significance to Eva Perón's identification with the Peronist workers.

Practically, they meant that, while her husband had to take over the task of governing by reconciling and deploying the different forces, contradictory interests, and ideologies represented among his followers, Evita's representation of the workers became exclusive and uncompromising within a movement whose official structure was no longer exclusively and uncompromisingly theirs. To the militant sectors of the masses of labourers who formed the popular support of Peronism, Evita often represented more than a person acting in their defence: to them she embodied the Peronist principle institutionalized for this purpose. Her very presence guaranteed their rights, and the fact that she was the wife of the leader of the party guaranteed her presence. Thus the characteristic duties she assumed and her specially militant way of fulfilling them formed an integral part of the movement: a specific way of aggressively representing the particular interests of the lowest strata of Argentinian society. These interests do not often coincide, they feel, with those of the class of labour leaders and party bureaucrats who took over the syndicate centre, the CGT, during the years of Peronist domination of the labour scene. 'In her representation of the workers, Eva Perón was in herself a complete and separate institution,' stated an intellectual activist of Peronism of the Bases, an underground group which identifies itself as a grass-roots organization, 'she was all that the CGT should have been but never was. The CGT is a sell-out, a farce.'

For Peronists who subscribe to an image of a revolutionary Eva, the weakness of bureaucratization implied that Evita's total identification with the masses and the way in which she lived this position constituted her own major contributions to Peronism. Peronists today feel that Eva acted as a radicalizing force at a time when the movement contained no formal statement of a radical ideology. This stood in apparent contradiction to the rest of the movement which, at the time, embarked on a policy of coexistence with, as well as conciliation of, conservative elements within the movement itself and outside it.

The accounts of Eva as the most radical of Peronist revolutionary elements depict her position of identification with the workers' cause and unfailing and uncompromising defence of it as a lonely stand shared not even with Perón himself. Perón defended this sector of his party in another way: through official channels, he needed to compromise and bargain with other groups in order to reach the final goal of defending and furthering the progress of the masses. He would never put at stake the interests of the working class for whose sake his negotiations had all been made. But Perón, unlike Eva, would bargain.

Today, thinking in retrospect, Peronists who consider themselves part of the ideological vanguard of their movement suggest that a great part of Eva's importance derives from this special position in relation to Perón. They feel that in the formative years of the history of Peronism virtually no one in the party, not even Perón, could introduce or develop the elements of the ideological position that Eva acted out with increasing conviction and originality day by day. Such a version points out that the Argentinian Left had early allied itself with anti-Peronism, due to cultural as well as political motives. This, it continues, stranded the new labour movement with few theoreticians and fewer members prepared to be receptive to the theory of a radical Left even had it existed as it does today within

Peronism. The Peronist masses could not always grasp the formulations of Socialist or Communist movements, which seemed to be based on experience and ideas foreign to many native-born Argentinians. But they could understand and identify with Eva Perón's life experience and could therefore follow her in the intuitive militancy that grew gradually and naturally from her past and her personality.

UNINSTITUTIONALIZED POWER

Immediately after the 17th of October, Juan Perón and Eva Duarte were married. Perón's attitude towards his young mistress consisted a political position, and Peronists who advocate Eva's militant alternative within Peronism interpret it as such. They recall that he made no secret of his unacceptable liaison with an unacceptable type of woman. He not only made her his mistress in the face of open disapproval of his military colleagues; he gave her a job and encouraged her to follow her own unconventional intuitions. When he later made her his bride, he confirmed and carried further his initial attitude. Upon assuming the presidency, Perón allowed his wife to claim that wherever she appeared with her unorthodox initiatives and ideas, she must be received as though unconditionally supported by Perón and his orthodox and irrefutable power. 'Wherever I am,' the twenty-six year old bleached blonde in her unpretentious Spanish could state, 'Perón is present.' And because he never contradicted this outrage, Perón admitted Eva, her impulses, and her actions as part of his own carefully calculated politics.

Eva Perón's revolutionary Peronism arose, then, from the experience of a youth and early adulthood like that of the working masses, a special intuitive perception of human nature and social injustice, a violently extremist personality, and a unique chain of circumstantial events. In these terms some Peronists account for her special leadership of their movement's militant sectors. They weigh all these elements—planned and fortuitous, personal and political, historical and ideological—as factors of equal importance and of a similar order. Because of this, some Peronists criticize the analysis of the ideology of Eva Perón as a mistaken endeavour of the intellectual sectors of Peronism alone. They believe that the 'ideologization' of her is a dehumanizing influence that cannot capture her personal and political richness.

To Peronists who hold up her revolutionary nature as exemplary, Eva Perón's distinctive approach towards life as a whole played a more important part in the formation of her radical stand than did most specific actions or formulations of ideas. Her followers, when referring to Evita's militancy, do not often think of certain consciously planned deeds or doctrines, but rather of her character and life in general. The relatively small importance they accord to her arms purchase and plans to arm the Argentinian workers illustrates this attitude. The Argentinian people have had access for the last few years to the facts of an apparent attempt by Eva on her deathbed to arm a Worker's Militia. This would seem to an outsider to offer the definitive evidence of the radical position of the Peronist First Lady. The incident, however, has not functioned as essential to the image of a revolutionary Eva Perón, though its increasing diffusion in many books and articles over the past years may in the end increase its importance. Nevertheless, it is significant that in early 1972 militant Peronists among factory workers who were convinced of Evita's revolutionary character and role did not know of the incident and furthermore refused to believe it.

Peronists often express awareness that the anti-Peronist rejection of Peronist politics and ideology might not so easily have become total and even violent had Eva Perón not existed as an intolerable element in Perón's barely tolerable façade. Anti-Peronism, according to this idea, could have put up with Juan Perón. His training was traditional; his rank was acceptable; his route to power was, for the most part, conventional. His political strategy tended to use normal channels and categories. But 'that woman' was unbearable, and her past was unforgiveable: she came directly from a profession, a family, and a whole life representing values unredeemed by preparation or participation in traditional hierarchies and in shocking contradiction to the values of established society. The question of whether or not Eva ever wished to be accepted by Argentinian society members of the radical Left in Peronism deem unimportant because they consider such acceptance to have been impossible. Eve Perón, they feel, could not deny her past; and Argentinian society would not forget it. [8]

And, they continue, while Eva could not change her past, she would not change her present loyalties. One or the other might perhaps have been grudgingly borne; both together were anathema. She made obvious to her enemies that Peronism would tolerate the lowest professions, the most shocking lack of education, the least acceptable family background. Peronists who subscribe to the versions of Eva's life that portray her as a revolutionary charge that anti-Peronism had supposed that Perón would keep these elements under control. He could give rights to the workers, but to the honourable workers— those who had been assimilated into established society through the channels of education, bureaucratic standards, electoral processes, institutionalized positions.[9] Eva Perón destroyed this illusion.

To the anti-Peronists she represented the most despised elements of the working masses, and yet Perón, far from holding her in check and forcing her to conform to established norms, allowed her to erupt into the highest spheres of power. There she exercised authority seen as illegitimate because it was apparently uncontrolled and blatantly uninstitutionalized. Wherever Eva Perón appeared, there appeared with her the danger that the class of people she represented could intrude as well. This intrusion was completely unacceptable to traditional sectors of Argentinian society, especially the military and the aristocracy, and Evita was dramatically cut off from conventional forces of the centre as well as from more conservative tendencies of the Right. Because of this Eva Perón, and the entire Peronist movement—from which it was impossible to disassociate her —was left in an increasingly radical position.

GUARDIAN OF PURITY

Those Peronists who see Eva as a revolutionary remember that the Eva they envisage and the process of radicalization that they suppose she inspired was not welcomed throughout the Peronist movement. They recall the increasing violence of her speeches and writings, in which she proclaimed herself the special guardian (*vigia*) of the Peronist revolution. But according to her revolutionary followers, she was their staunchest bulwark not only against anti-Peronism, but also against betrayals of the Peronist cause within the movement itself.

Her role as guard, standing watch over the purity of the revolution, receives careful attention and elaboration in militant Peronist versions of her life. These versions often describe her role in terms of her personality. Eva, for example, was widely believed to be far more sceptical about human beings in general than her husband was. In this interpretation, Juan Perón, being the theoretician and strategist of his movement, judged people on logical and practical grounds, concerned mainly with their usefulness to Peronism. In contrast, Eva displayed remarkable intuition about the people around her and based her conclusions about the value of each person on feelings rather than on rational grounds. In her almost religious enthusiasm—which she herself proudly termed fanaticism—for the ends of a 'pure' movement, she judged Peronists not so much by their usefulness but by their fidelity to the movement and to Perón. Relying on her intuition, Eva often denounced the very groups that Perón was simultaneously conciliating and using.[10]

Her very fanaticism and intransigence provoked resistance from the groups within Peronism which she opposed. For many it was this resistance that shaped events in Eva's life after October 17, 1945. They claim that the 'comfortable' Peronists—middle class party members, many labour leaders, and the vast party bureaucracy—feared her extremism. It is said that even as they used Eva for purposes of propaganda, their resistance became more forceful and obstinate. Resentment grew as Eva participated more and more directly in Peronist politics, influencing the leadership, the goals of action and even the basic ideological orientation of the entire movement. Many Peronists today suggest that people within the movement blocked her projects and ideas. Eva, they say, was not intimidated, but became bolder in her warnings against the oligarchic spirit within Peronism itself, warnings that have become among the passages most remembered and most often cited from Eva Perón's work.

RENUNCIATION

The conflict came briefly into the open during the episode of the Renunciation, when Evita received the nomination as candidate for the vice-presidency and then declined it. Some Peronists, in explaining her refusal, give equal importance to the usual accounts of pressure from the military and to new versions of resistance and even intrigue among the Peronist bureaucracy and middle class. Others see these opposing groups as latent forces in a continuing struggle made obvious in the Renunciation. At that time, according to these accounts, a final break was made and sides were drawn up for a confrontation that was to last beyond the death of its main protagonist.

None of these interpretations suggests that it might have been desirable for Eva to occupy the vice-presidency. Rather, Peronists pushing their movement toward revolution condemn the idea that Eva should institutionalize her significance within Peronism by assuming a conventional post in a conventional bureaucracy. Such an appointment would have made obvious the fact that a Peronist Party had left behind the original spontaneity of the Peronist movement. Many believe therefore, that with the Renunciation Eva declared her revolutionary identity in its most convincing and mature form. Her open alignment with the workers and their cause stated definitively the radical nature of her version of Peronism. Though differences of opinion on the question of whether or not Eva could have freely chosen to accept or reject the candidacy do exist among radical Peronists, their interpretations of the results of her final refusal of honour and office generally coincide. In the *Renunciamiento*, these versions claim, the processes begun on October 17, 1945 reached a climax: a sycophantic and conservative bureaucracy finally won the upper hand in the party as an institution, and the identity of Eva Perón merged with that of the anonymous masses who were unrepresented in Argentinian society and only poorly represented in the Peronist movement. Many of her followers today proclaim these processes, completed in 1951, as key to the figure of Eva Perón and her significance. At that time, they assert, she renounced all ambitions and all pretensions to bureaucratic office and institutionalized power. Never again could her enemies accuse her of ambition. Her sacrifice placed her irrefutably and eternally alongside her followers in the intra-party conflict, which has grown in intensity over the years. Eva Perón wanted nothing. More important, she *was* nothing: she renounced her claim to power and position and return to the anonymity of her beloved *descamisados*.

Less than a year later she was dead, and the corruption within Peronism burst out of control. Bureaucratic and opportunistic elements moved into a position of dominance, which they held until the fall of Perón in 1955. Eva Perón's ideology suffered the fate of her corpse: the purity of her Peronism was violated and cast aside, only to be restored after years of cleansing hardship and violence.

CONCLUSIONS

The image of an aggressive and violent female revolutionary seems
to be in direct opposition to the ideal that places women on an
exclusively feminine domestic throne, from which she exercises a
power alien to the forms of public office and rational thought. The
warrior Eva felt no need to keep her action from the public arena, nor
to disguise the reality of her power behind a façade of female domesticity. But her followers nevertheless describe her in terms of more
orthodox femininity: themes of passivity, self-sacrifice, emotion and
irrationality, as well as lack of legitimated or institutionalized power,
come into focus in the images of the revolutionary heroine.

In her relations with her husband, the leader, as well as with the
Peronist following, the Revolutionary Eva Perón's role was passive.
Perón formed her, using her unique qualities; the masses revealed a
new mode of action to her on the 17th of October and thus provided
her distinctive identity. Her self-effacement before her husband and
followers, and her sacrifice for them, reached their culmination, as
explicitly stated by Peronist militants, in the Renunciation of the
vice-presidency. The Renunciation had a further significance: Evita
chose an unofficial role within Peronism, confirming the fact that
she could not and would not hold institutionalized power and legitimate authority. This she had long expressed in her proudly emotional, disorderly, 'fanatic'[11] action, contrasted with Perón's calculated and scientific use of traditional forms of official power.

Three elements of the conventional feminine ideal are not elaborated here, but may be significant in their absence. Descriptions of the
Revolutionary Eva do not stress her maternal nature, her beauty, or
her chastity. One can assume that the idea of motherhood, associated
with an entirely domestic sphere, would remove Eva from the role of
companion in battle and from the public arena in which the action
had to take place. As *compañera* in the guerrilla, Eva was devoid of
childlike and saintly qualities. Yet the very lack of emphasis on her
physical appearance enhances the impression of her as an asexual
being, and consistently, her sexual purity is not stressed. Ideas about
her relationship with her husband reinforce this impression: they
are formulated in terms of companionship and frequently are
phrased in an entirely ideological idiom.

Further, Eva's role as guardian of the purity of the Peronist movement is relevant. Versions of the Revolutionary Eva do not designate this role as distinctly feminine. Nevertheless, it cannot be seen in isolation from the definition of a similar role as the special domain of womanhood in the myths of orthodox Peronism, which portray the maintenance of the morality of the home as special feminine tasks.

Peronists subscribing to the image of a militant Eva often incorporated elements of it into their own behaviour. The passive submission to Perón in the hope that he, in his enigmatic dealings from Madrid, would structure and use their special qualities was an attitude frequently encountered in revolutionary Peronism. Radicals of this persuasion saw this situation as similar to Evita's: their special contribution was rejected by other sectors of their movement but accepted by Perón himself, who understood it better even than those who offered it.

New militant, often intellectual, Peronists discarded most of the status symbols of orthodox Peronism's propaganda. But they preserved ideas of an intuitive and emotionally fanatic Eva Perón and of an equally intuitive and emotional popular response to her.[12] They claimed that their attitude to the phenomenon of Eva was based not on an intellectual recognition of her ideological position, but on an instinctive grasp of the woman's personality traits and emotional style: 'You cannot analyse Eva Perón'. Professional academics in the new ranks of leftist Peronism assumed this attitude, questioning their own careers, and construing very literally the popular Peronist slogan 'Workshoes, yes! Books, no!' Eva's ideas were unimportant in as much as she made no important formulations of them. Her followers emulated her personal example; they did not study her doctrine.

Peronism of the Left, then, rejected orderly, official, and 'rational' institutions and plans and espoused the emotional, intuitive mode of action thought to be Eva's, as well as being characteristic of her popular following. In all of this the followers of the Revolutionary Eva, like those who believe in Lady of Hope or the woman of the Black Myth, link these traits with a woman and with the masses. They associate an uninstitutionalized power based on these traits with revolutionary leadership.

The image of Eva as revolutionary, which recombines the elements of her culture's feminine ideal, offers more than a new option for women. These factors, personified by the radical warrior image and associated with femininity in other contexts, define a role explicitly and unqualifiedly available to men as well as to women. This Eva Perón opts for none of the types of power suggested as characteristic of women. She enters neither a male role nor an exclusively male world; she does not exploit a domestic position or use unique female qualities to stress her differences from men. She uses culturally defined, characteristically female attributes as a basis for power in a role accessible to both males and females, and is able to do this because the definition of a revolutionary role includes elements congruent with feminine values. As an emulated leader in this role, whether she creates or discovers it, a woman recruits both female and male followers. Without stressing her unique female identity and without entering a male world, she opens to herself the possibility of undisguised power.

8

Conclusions

It is possible that many cultures link images of feminine nature with certain types of mystical power, and with revolutionary roles. This work has investigated in detail one case that demonstrates such symbolic logic.

The Lady of Hope and the woman of the Black Myth make positive and negative statements of the same feminine ideal. The woman who fulfills this ideal finds her action limited to a domestic realm and an irrational mode. Within these limits any power she may exercise is likewise outside the formal structures of society and of reason. Both myths, directly or indirectly, praise the woman whose feminine sexuality provides her with her identity and her ultimate goals in life. Yet because these are limited to the vocations of wife and mother, she must guard her purity carefully. Her physical drives or their emotional concomitants lead her to the one man who bestows her wifely and maternal roles on her, and who, because of her continuing love for him, directs her in these and all other aspects of her existence. Her emotional sensibilities and her special intuition govern her unerring taste and sensitivity to beauty, and in response to them she cultivates the arts and her own appearance. Because of her femininity, then, she depends entirely on instinct and emotion, and consequently on her husband and his decisions. Neither her own mind nor the protocols and rules of society outside the home motivate or direct her. Her appearance reflects all these aspects of her quintessential womanhood. Her face and figure express dependence and childlike purity, while her bearing and elegance could not have been learned and can result only from instinctive taste.

The Black Myth makes its statement of this ideal by explicitly damning a woman who expresses its opposite. Active and self-assertive, such a woman too is driven by irrational impulses, but, uncontrolled, her emotions erupt only in violence and in the indulgence of her bestial instincts. They lead her to a scandalous promiscuity, the negation of chaste domesticity; to flagrant disregard for formality and rank. She is grossly incapable of comprehending the delicate nuances of culture, the realms of good taste and fine art. All her efforts to hide her true nature cannot compensate for her lack of aesthetic sense or of purity: nothing will suffice to render her lovely.

Inherently involved with domesticity, alien to office, strategy, and even intellect, the ideal woman exercises power, but only a power qualified by this definition of her femininity. In this position, this woman has an influence that is beyond analysis: not political, but spiritual, mystical, irrational. When properly esconced in a domestic situation, a woman's physical and emotion nature exercises a beneficial influence over her immediate family, or over those people, however many they are, who relate to her as members of her immediate family. In the domestic context men can limit her sexuality. But if a female rejects her domestic vocation and with it masculine control over her sexuality, then her power, out of control, becomes illegitimate and malevolent.

Because it is unanalysable and directly related to instinct and emotion, this power, whether evil or good, attracts and fascinates those sectors of society believed to be incapable of intellectual analysis because of their own total subjection to their physical and emotional drives. In place of a reasoned political allegiance, the masses offer a mystic and fanatical adoration to the woman who has legitimately assumed or illegitimately imposed her power over them. Because she exercises an influence that owes nothing to existing social forms and attracts a following marginal to these forms, such a woman is a revolutionary by definition.

The myth of the Revolutionary Eva Perón does not define her as the incarnation of the feminine ideal. But it does describe her in terms that recall the ideal woman in the myths espoused by both anti-Peronism and Peronist orthodoxy. This woman depends on her emotions and instincts to lead her to accept the guidance of her husband, or, at other times, of her people. Although she is not confined to the domestic scene, she sacrifices office and honours. She acts outside the frameworks and categories of society and of intellectual analysis, attracting a following which obeys intuition and emotion, not reason, to fight at her side. The myth may de-emphasize her femininity, but it is no accident that this revolutionary is a woman.

In the images examined, the three elements consistently linked—femininity, mystical or spiritual power, and revolutionary leadership—display an underlying common theme. Identification with any one of these elements puts a person or a group at the margins of established society and at the limits of institutionalized authority. Anyone who can identify with all three images lays an overwhelming and echoing claim to dominance through forces that recognize no control in society or its rules. Only a woman can embody all three elements of this power. Herein may lie the key to the central significance of Eva Perón for the Argentinian middle classes.

But Eva may lay yet another claim to her sway over the forces that society cannot encompass. At the time I carried out these investigations, the Argentinians—both her enemies and her followers—saw not only a woman. They saw a corpse. The repeated emphasis on the different versions of her death and in the constant concern with the fate of her remains were inescapable. The fact that Eva's body had not been buried was an important and disturbing issue for politicians and popular groups, while official propaganda openly exploited parallels with Christian hagiography.

Westerners need not turn to other cultures to find ideologies that construe death as a source of power and a sign of proximity to the divine. Such conceptualizations in funerary and initiation rites of non-Western cultures[1] have been used to illuminate similar ideas in the Christian traditions of the West. In her martyrdom, Eva associates herself with spiritual power in the form of the sanctity that Christianity granted its martyrs in their elect place in the company of saints. Her intact body parallels the identical symbol of sanctity and triumph over death of other saints and martyrs.[2] Even in social sectors unresponsive to Peronist propaganda, or in those disassociated from the church (as in the case of some adherents of the Revolutionary myth of Eva), it would be difficult, given the influence of Roman Catholicism in Argentina, for these associations to fail to find some resonance.

Such reflections of hagiography and of imagery associated with death may be seen in other instances of uninstutitionalized spiritual power: for example, that of Che Guevara and of Bandaranaike of Sri Lanka. The cultures differ widely, but in both cases followers associated their dead heroes with saintly martyrdom and with spiritual leadership.

Eva Perón exercised a power seen by friends and enemies alike as spiritual or mystical, uninstitutionalized and irrational—a power exhibiting characteristics that coincide with the definition of her feminine nature. To some extent her continuing importance and popularity may be attributed not only to her power as a woman but also to the power of the dead. However a society's vision of the after-life may be structured, death by its nature remains a mystery, and, until society formally allays the commotion it causes, a source of disturbance and disorder. Women and the dead—death and woman-hood—stand in similar relation to structured social forms: outside public institutions, unlimited by official rules, and beyond formal categories. As a female corpse reiterating a symbolic theme as both woman and martyr, Eva Perón perhaps lays a double claim to spiritual leadership.

Notes

To facilitate smooth reading, when possible the references for closely related points made within a paragraph have been cited together in one note at the end of the paragraph. Works in such a note are cited in the same order as the points to which they refer appear in the text. Material that originally appeared in Spanish has been translated by the author, unless otherwise noted.

INTRODUCTION

1. Popularized versions of a saintly Eva and her mystically fanatic following appear, for example, in *Barnes*, e.g. 76, 121, 136, 167, 175, 177, *Naipul* (1972a), and *Sacquard de Belleroche* (e.g., 77 (note), 173, 175, 208), as well as in Radley Metzger's film 'Little Mother' (Audobon Films, 1973) and the rock opera 'Evita' by Tim Rice and Andrew Webber (1977).

    Examples of more serious works referring to a similar interpretation of Evita and her popularity are *Bourne* (278, 279, 283), *Hennessy* (33, 55, note 8), and *Lux Wurm* (Ch. IX).

CHAPTER 1

1. Interview, 1972.
2. *Perón, E.*, 1951: 63.
3. *Crisostomo*, 1970: 200–201; 208.
4. Dr. A. Namika Raby first pointed out to me the possibility of parallels between the Perón and the Bandaranaike cases. I owe not only the original inspiration for this comparison, but also most of the information on which it is based, to her.

5. See *Ortner*, 1973 and *Rosaldo*, 1973.
6. *Ortner*, 1973; *Rosaldo*, 1973: 30–31.
7. *Rosaldo*, 1973: 21, 29–30 quoting *Bateson*, 1958: 253; *Landes*, 1971: v; and *Paul*, 1973.
8. *Rosaldo*, 1973: 37–38, 42.
9. See *Shack*, 1966.
10. See *Barth*, 1959.
11. See *Coomaraswamy*, 1942.
12. 1961, 18–25.
13. *Coomaraswamy*, 1942: 1–10, 26–72, 50–53.
14. See *Harper* and *Wadley*, 1975: 121; 1977; *Coomaraswamy*, 1942: 69.
15. *Faron*, 1964: 8, 192–206.
16. Ibid., 158.
17. *Harper*, 1969.
18. *Douglas*, 1977: 141, 128, 133, 72, 57, 99, 71. See also *Cott*, 1977.
19. *Pescatello*, 1973.
20. *Witke*, 1977: 330, 342–343, 345.

CHAPTER 2

1. See, for example, her speech of 25 April 1947.
2. See *Halperín*, 1970: 9–24, quoting Irazusta, 2.
3. *Sarmiento*, 1970: 161–162.
4. Ibid., 40, 41, 141.
5. Ibid., 160.
6. Ibid., 91, 102, quoting twice Alex, *Histoire de l'empire ottoman*.
7. Ibid., 207.
8. Ibid., 195.

CHAPTER 3

1. *Radiolandia*, 7 April 1945: 25–29.
2. *Roberto Pettinato*, personal communication.
3. *Borroni and Vacca*, 1970: 75, citing Radio Belgrano, broadcasts for the week of 23 June 1944: 'Hacia un futuro mejor'. Libretto: Muñoz Azpiri.
4. *Panorama*, 21 April 1970: 67.

5. *Borroni and Vacca*, 1970: 79–80, citing 'various magazines', 9 November 1944.
6. *Luna*, 1971: 337–338.
7. *Borroni and Vacca*, 1970: 129–131; *La Prensa*, 9 February 1946: 6; *Tribuna Demócrata*, 13 February 1946: 5.
8. *Democracia*, 27 November 1946: 9; 28 November 1946: 5.
9. Ibid., 19 March 1946: 3, 4, 5.
10. *Tribuna Demócratica*, 5 March 1947: 6.
11. Ibid., 12 March 1947: 6; 19 March 1947: 2.
12. *Democracia*, 27 May 1948, Section 2:1.
13. *Tribuna Demócrata*, 21 August 1946: 3; *La Vanguardia*, 13 May 1947: 6.
14. *Borroni and Vacca*, 1970: 166, citing Eva Perón, Radio Argentina broadcast 11 June 1947.
15. *Primera Plana*, 27 December 1966: 37.
16. Ibid., 13 December 1966: 40; *Congressional Record*, 26–27 June 1947; *Borroni and Vacca*, 1970: 135.
17. *Borroni and Vacca*, 1970: 169.
18. *Primera Plana*, 22 October 1968: 61; *Democracia*, 28 July 1951: 3.
19. *Democracia*, 29 August 1948: 3; 7 December 1948: 1.

It is not unusual in Argentina for a married woman to be known simply by her name and husband's surname, unaccompanied by either her maiden surname or the 'de' which customarily precedes the husband's surname in Spanish. Nevertheless, the credit for the 'invention' of the name Eva Perón is claimed as an honour both by Raúl Apold (personal communication) and by Roberto Pettinato for Francisco Muñoz Azpiri (personal communication). Both figures, who were of importance in the creation and maintenance of the public image of Eva Perón, seem to feel that the shortening of the name was a significant contribution to the formation of her political identity.

Primera Plana cites September, 1950 as the date of Eva's choice to shorten her name. The author apparently links the decision with the official change of the name of the Fundación 'María Eva Duarte de Perón' (17 December 1966: 37b). The short name Eva Perón appeared even earlier than the date cited in the present work. *Democracia* used it in two articles concerning the admiration of the Brazilian woman for the Argentine First Lady. Since the articles involved quotes and thus translations from the

Portuguese, and since their example was not followed by other reports, they may be considered unrepresentative (*Democracia*, 17 January 1947: 5; 18 January 1947: 5).

20. *El Hogar*, 7 November 1947: 28–29.
21. *Borroni and Vacca*, 1970: 205–208.
22. *Primera Plana*, 27 December 1966: 38.
23. *La Nación*, 20 September 1951: 4; *Democracia*, 26 January 1946: 11; 21 September 1951: 1.
24. *Primera Plana*, 27 December 1966: 37b–38.
25. *Democracia*, 6 December 1951: 3.
26. *Baily*, 1967: 131; *Bourne*, 1970: 268.
27. *Arciniegas*, 1956: 58; *Borroni and Vacca*, 1970: 250; *Flores*, 1952: 233.
28. November 1950: 16; December 1950: 2.
29. *Borroni and Vacca*, 1970: 249–250.
30. *Democracia*, 6 December 1950: 3; 7 December 1950: 3.
31. *Baily*, 1967: 100.
32. *La Vanguardia*, 18 January 1946: 2; 5 August 1947: 3; *Borroni and Vacca*, 1970: 202.
33. *Primera Plana*, 10 January 1967: 36; 7 May 1968: 69, 71; 20 December 1966: 71b.
34. *Arciniegas*, 1956: 59, citing H. L. Matthews in the *New York Times*.
35. *Primera Plana*, 10 January 1967: 36; *Borroni and Vacca*, 1970: 243–245.
36. *Democracia*, 15 July 1950; 15 May 1951: 1; 16 May 1951: 3; 19 May 1951: 3.
37. *Ciria*, 1971: 116; Gallo, personal communication.
38. *Perón, J.*, 1971, 135–136.
39. *Perón, J.*, 1970b: 66.
40. *Borroni and Vacca*, 1970: 126.
41. *Bourne*, 266–268; *Main*, 188–189; cf., *Primera Plana*, 24 January 1967: 38 quoting Penella de Silva.
42. *Peña*, 1971: 110; *Main*, 116.
43. *Borroni and Vacca*, 1970: 267–268.
44. Ibid., 213, citing Eva Perón: January 1949.
45. Ibid., 242.
46. *Primera Plana*, 27 September 1966: 39.
47. *Borroni and Vacca*, 1970: 243.
48. *Primera Plana*, 10 January 1967: 37a–38b.
49. This description is based on the transcription made by *Borroni*

and Vacca, 260–264, of the recordings preserved in the Museum of the Word, General Archives of the Nation.

50. *Primera Plana*, 10 January 1967: 38b.
51. *Borroni and Vacca*, 1970: 259.
52. *Primera Plana*, 10 January 1967: 38.
53. *Borroni and Vacca*, 1970: 268–272.
54. Ibid., 274.
55. *Democracia*, 14 March 1952: 1.
56. Ibid., 6 April 1952: 1, 3; *Borroni and Vacca*, 277.
57. *Borroni and Vacca*, 1970: 278–284.
58. Ibid., 287–289.
59. Ibid., 284, 287–290.
60. Ibid., 292–293.
61. *Arciniegas*, 1956: 99.
62. *Borroni and Vacca*, 1970: 317.
63: *Viñas*, 1965b: 20; *Democracia*, 4–6 April 1952.
64. Apold, personal communication.
65. *Democracia*, 1 August 1952: 1.
66. *Borroni and Vacca*, 1970: 320–321.
67. *Sebreli*, 1966: 155.
68. *Borroni and Vacca*, 1970: 329; *Primera Plana*, 28 May 1968, 48; *Baily*, 1967: 150.
69. *Sebreli*, 1966: 156.
70. *Borroni and Vacca*, 1970: 287.
71. See *Baily*, who traces this theme in the publicity of the CGT from the days following Eva's death to the month before the fall of Perón in 1955: 147–148, 154, 159.
72. *Borroni and Vacca*, 1970: 334–336.
73. Ibid., 337.
74. Fiscalía Nacional de Recuperación Patrimonial and the Comisión Liquidadora Decreto Ley 8124/57.
75. *García*, 1971: 431, citing Percy Foster in the *Herald Examiner* of Los Angeles, 4 May 1970.
76. Percy Foster, personal communication.
77. *Borroni and Vacca*, 1970: 287.
78. Ibid., 338–339.
79. Ibid., 339–340.
80. Ibid., 340.

81. Ibid., 240–341.
82. *La Opinión*, 7 September 1971: 24, citing notes and acts of the SIE.

CHAPTER 4

1. *Murray*, 1971: no page.
2. *Perón, E.*, 1951: 65, 59, 261, 263–264.
3. Ibid., 45–47 (italics mine), 1971: 144.
4. 27 August 1947.
5. 208.
6. 1951: 74.
7. *Democracia*, 19 October 1951: 8.
8. Interview, 1970.
9. *Democracia*, 8 October 1951: 2.
10. *Tribuna Demócrata*, 1 January 1947: 1.
11. *Tribuna Demócrata*, 27 November 1946: 6.
12. *Tribuna Demócrata*, 12 February 1947.
13. *Tribuna Demócrata*, 30 April 1947: 2.
14. *Tribuna Demócrata*, 4 June 1947: 6.
15. *Tribuna Demócrata*, 2 July 1947: 5.
16. *Walsh*, 1965: 21. This remarkable fictional account of an interview with a member of the commando that buried Eva Perón coincides with many of the facts made available after the exhumation of the body in 1971.

CHAPTER 5

1. The reader will note that the sources cited here for the Black Myth represent different political traditions. This is justified in part because the Democratic Alliance included apparently disparate parties, which reconciled their differences in order to oppose Perón. It may be objected, however, that criticism aimed at Eva from the Left, as in the cases, for example, of *La Vanguardia* and authors such as Franco, springs from a context of a tradition of criticism of bourgeois values which might be characterized as an ethic of the Left. Thus, the criticisms of Eva's material extravagance may be interpreted as the perception of the political and ideological inconsistency that her

appearance and possessions represented. This is, of course, a qualification which must be borne in mind. But it would seem to be minimized by the fact that such criticism possibly based on ideological conviction is, as may be seen throughout this chapter, similar to that of more conservative versions of the Black Myth and, more importantly still, found in the context of a similar set of other values. Such is the case of the censure on Eva's sexuality or lack of erudition, for example, which comes from the Left as well as from the Right. Significant also is the lack of perception during the Perón decade of any coincidence between Eva's political views or action and those of the Left. Repetto's attempt to draw attention to such a congruence (1952) was severely reproached by fellow Socialists. Further, the Argentinian Left has since gradually modified its opinion of Eva Perón, as emphasized here in Chapter 7, to the extent that some groups of Marxist origin or conviction have completely reversed their views. It may be of importance to remark that in these cases the supposed clashes between Eva's attitudes or appearance with any political ethic have been disregarded, which might suggest that they were never of primary importance. However, further investigation into this point will be necessary before any definitive conclusions may be drawn, especially concerning opinion in the Left in Argentina today.

2. Interview, 1970.
3. *Raggi*, 12; *Gillone*, 138.
4. 1951: 315.
5. *Borroni and Vacca*, 1970: 302, quoting Delia Parodi.
6. *Costanzo*, 1948: 56.
7. *El Laborista*, 4 August 1952: no page. Colección Peronista, Library of Congress, Buenos Aires: Recortes periodísticos diversos.
8. *Tejada and Zubillaga*, 1953a: 65.
9. Plate conceived by Napoleón Solleza and executed by E. Meliante, 1952 for the Sindicato de Vendedores de Diarios, Revistas y Afines: Colección Peronista, Library of Congress, Buenos Aires. Dr. Noreen Stack first drew my attention to this uncatalogued document and later kindly made a reproduction of it available to me.
10. E. g., *Langer*, 1966: 99; *Martínez Estrada*, 1956: 246–247; *Naipul*, 1972a: 6.

11. *Burgin*, 1970: 136, quoting Jorge Luis Borges.
12. Interview, 1970.
13. *Main*, 1956: 70–71.
14. *Boizard*, 1955: 128–130.
15. Interview, 1971.
16. *Perón, E.*, 1951: 63.
17. *Democracia*, 1 November 1946: 3; 1 December 1946: 1.
18. *Democracia*, 9 August 1952: 1; 5 August 1952: 1.
19. *Democracia*, 5 August 1952: 1; 19 August 1952: 1.
20. *Democracia*, 14 January 1950: 3.
21. *Democracia*, 14 February 1951: 1.
22. *Perón, E.*, 1951: 278, 305.
23. *Democracia*, 14 December 1946: 5; 28 November 1946: 3; 19 February 1948: 9; 30 November 1946: 3; 14 December 1946: 5; 31 December 1946: 5.
24. *Democracia*, 23 November 1947: 5.
25. *El Hogar*, August, 1952: 11.
26. *Democracia*, 22 February 1952: 3; 7 March 1952: 1.
27. *Democracia*, 18 June 1951: 1; 17 December 1949: 3.
28. *Langer*, 1966: 100–103.
29. 1951: 61–62, 274, 30, 245.
30. Ibid., 1951: 47.
31. *Democracia*, 13 January 1950: 1.
32. *Democracia*, 13 January 1950: 1; 18 October 1951: 2.
33. *Democracia*, 15 December 1948: 1; 2 May 1950: 8, 27 June 1952: 4; 18 October 1951: 2.
34. *Democracia*, 27 July 1952: 2; 27 July 1952: 8.
35. *Democracia*, 21 June 1952: 2; 31 July 1952: 3; - October 1951: 2; Apold, personal communication.
36. *Democracia*, 8 May 1952: 1; 15 May 1952: 1.
37. *Tribuna Demócrata*, 3 August 1946: last page; 28 August 1946: 6; *La Vanguardia*, 11 March 1947, Supplement, *Vanguardia Feminina*: no page.
38. *La Vanguardia*, 5 November 1946: 1; 24 December 1946; 3 June 1947: 4.
39. Interview, 1971.
40. *Democracia*, 26 June 1947: 3; *Murray*, 1971: no page; *Tejada and Zubillaga*, 1953b: 58.
41. *Raggi*, 1953: 12.

42. *Las Bases*, 23 November 1971: 19.

43. *Tribuna Demócrata*, 4 June 1947: 6; *Lombille*, 1956: 60; *Main*, 1956: 79; *Copi*, 1970: no page; *Eloy Martínez*, 1970a: 44.

44. *Radiolandia*, 3 June 1944: 26–28; *Ahora*, 10 July 1947: cover, 11–12; 15 July 1947: cover, 11; 17 July 1947: 4–5.

45. *Murray*, 1971: no page; *Martínez Payva and Rivero*, 1970: Vol. 2, 191.

46. *Tribuna Demócrata*, 5 March 1947: 6.

47. *Ghioldi*, 1956: 54.

48. *Democracia*, 3 September 1947: 3.

49. *Democracia*, 30 May 1948: 3; 27 July 1952: 5.

50. *Democracia*, 28 December 1950: 4.

51. *Democracia*, 30 May 1948: 3.

52. *Perón, E.*, 1951: 193–194, 122.

53. *Democracia*, 23 August 1951: 5.

54. *Franco*, 1958: 150; *Main*, 1956: 121–124; *Ghioldi*, 1956: 51–53; *Acossano*, 1955: 100.

55. *Martínez Estrada*, 1956: 260; *Borroni and Vacca*, 1970: 114, quoting Colonel Gerardo Demetro, formerly of the Tenth Cavalry Unit, 1945, in his testimonial to *Primera Plana* 19 October 1965.

56. *Democracia*, 21 June 1952: 2; 31 July 1952: 3; 8 October 1951: 2.

57. *Democracia*, 18 March 1949: 3; *Rina Rodríguez*, 1949; *Tejada and Zubillaga*: 1953b: 42; *Branchini*, 1953: 26.

58. *Capitski*, 1968: 2; *Borroni and Vacca*, 1970: 223, citing Irma Cabrera de Ferrari.

59. *Tejada and Zubillaga*, 1953a: 1; *Aristondo*, 1949: 37; *La Razón*, 1 August 1952: no page; Colección Peronista, Library of Congress, Buenos Aires: Recortes periodísticos varios.

60. *Democracia*, 23 August 1947: 2; 18 March 1949: 3; *Perón, E.*, 1971: 9.

61. *Tejada and Zubillaga*, 1953b; *Tejada*, 1953a; *Mundo Infantil*, 4 August 1952: 1; see also *Mundo Infantil*, 4 August 1952: 43; 18 August 1952: cover; *Tejada and Zubillaga*, 1953b: 42; *Costanzo*, 1948: 29.

62. *Democracia*, 29 July 1952:6; 31 July 1952:6; 29 July 1952; 2: 3 August 1952: 2.

63. *Democracia*, 22 August 1952: 3.

64. *Ghioldi*, 1956: 54.

65. *Sánchez Zinny*, 1958: 98; *Ghioldi*, 1956: 24–26; *Libro Negro*, 1958: 43; *Lombille*, 1956: 133.

66. *Martínez Estrada*, 1956: 251.
67. *Ghioldi*, 1956: 60–61.
68. *Perón, E.*, 1951: 18, 126; 1971: 150.

CHAPTER 6

1. *Terragno*, 1971: 12.
2. According to the apologist for the Rosas regime, José María Rosa,

> The portrait was not set on the altar—as the anti-Rosists of Montevideo would say and as charged in the sentence of Rosas of 1858—Very little was lacking for the situation to reach this point, and of course, the desires for it to do so existed amongst the excited people. It was placed in the chancel 'on the Gospel side', which traditionally corresponded—and corresponds—to the heads of state. The portrait was treated as it was in banquets where it was given the place of honour and toasts were made to it as though Rosas himself were present.

On the same page Rosa gives this description of the Rosist regime's fostering of popular enthusiasm:

> The people's worship of the caudillo had reached idolatry. He was identified with the fatherland as Federalism was with religion. Bishop Medrano gave orders to the priests to preach that 'outside of Federalism, no religion is possible' (1964: Vol. IV, 402).

3. *Ramos Mejía*, 1927: Vol. 2, 17–27; *Ibarguren*, 1961: 211, 213; *Sánchez Zinny*, 1941: 197; *López*, 1957: Vol. VI, 178; Vol. VII, 696; *Iriarte*, 1947: Vol. 5, 202–203; *Rivera Indarte*, 1930: Vol. 2, 188; *Sarmiento*, 1970: 237.
4. *Muello*, 1916: 113.
5. *Sánchez Viamonte*, 1930: 79.
6. *Archinegas*, 1956: 79; *Sánchez Sorondo*, 1923: 163–165; *Corallini*, 1931: 261, citing *Crítica*, 25 January 1930: 5.
7. *Sánchez Sorondo*, 1923: 163–165; *Corallini*, 1931: 260–263.
8. *Corallini*, 1931: 258–259.
9. *Sánchez Viamonte*, 193?: 74; *López*, 1957: Vol. VII, 696; *Martínez Estrada*, 1956: 107, 253.

10. *Martínez Estrada*, 1956: 289.
11. *Viñas*, 1963b.
12. 127, 29, 50, 94, 130.
13. *Tribuna Demócrata*, 5 March 1947: 6.
14. *Mosca*, 1946: 81; *Tribuna Demócrata*, 4 December 1946: 5; 9 April 1947: 6.
15. 1946: 48, 49, 86, 127.
16. *Viñas*, 1963a: 50.
17. *Iriarte*, 1947: Vol. 5, 113; Interview, 1970.
18. *Ramos Mejía*, 1927: Vol. 2, 344–345.
19. *Wilde*, 1966.
20. 85.
21. *Sánchez Viamonte*, 1930: 105.
22. *Martínez Estrada*, 1956: 252–253; *Reyna Almandos*, 1920: 88; *Corallini*, 1931: 166–169.
23. *Reyna Almandos*, 1920: 107–108, 13, 131.
24. *Sánchez Viamonte*, 1930; *Reyna Almandos*, 1920: 338.
25. *Corallini*, 1931: 167–169; *Martínez Estrada*, 1956: 252.
26. *Corallini*, 1931: 161, 231, 281; *Reyna Almandos*, 1920: 183, 338; *Muello*, 1916: 53–54, citing *La Nación*; *Damonte Taborda*, 1955: 73.
27. *Reyna Almandos*, 1920: 299–329; *Sánchez Zinny*, 1941: 154–155; *Goldar*, 1971: 89–90, citing Jorgelina Loubet, *La breve curva* n.d., no page; *Mosca*, 1946: 49.
28. Imaz' brief examination of the values of the Argentinian upper classes suggests the value and definition of culture in the upper strata of Argentinian society. His work points out that 'culture' and 'education' [*instrucción*] comprise different categories but that the former is valued far more highly than the latter (1962: 45–47).
29. Obviously the sources cited here represent very different political traditions within anti-Peronism. However, again the context of the observations contained in note 1, Chapter 5 makes it possible to draw parallels between these expressions of different ideological positions.
30. *La Vanguardia*, 3 June 1947: 4; *Lombille*, 1956: 93; *Tribuna Demócrata*, 13 November 1946: 5.
31. 1946: 46, 81, 127, 49, 102, 65.
32. *Ramos Mejía*, 1927: Vol. I, 258–289; *Mármol*, 1887: Vol. I, 71–72 and *passim.*; *Iriarte*, 1947: Vol. 5, 72.

33. *Mansilla,* 121. Mansilla supported Rosas, his brother-in-law, but as a member of the upper class voiced anti-popular sentiment of the time.
34. Ibid., 121, 24.
35. *Ramos Mejía,* 1927: Vol. 2, 336–338; *Iriarte,* Vol. 5, 72.
36. Ibid., 336–338; *Mármol,* 1887, see also 1917: 41–43; *Sánchez Zinny,* 1942: 58.
37. *Mansilla,* 1925: 128–129.
38. *Ramos Mejía,* 1927: Vol. 2, 331; *Iriarte,* 1947: 72–73.
39. *Reyna Almandos,* 1920: 117; *Sánchez Viamonte,* 1930: 139–140.
40. Ibid., 21, 11; Ibid., 107; *Ayarragaray,* 1930: 96; *Villafañe,* 1922: 139–174.
41. *Sánchez Sorondo,* 1923: ix; *La Nación,* 12 October 1922: 4; *Reyna Almandos,* 1920: 21; *Martínez Estrada,* 1946: Vol. 1, 46; Vol. 2, 238
42. *Ayarragaray,* 1930: 147; *Reyna Almandos,* 1920: 20; *Sánchez Sorondo,* 1923: xvi; *Sánchez Viamonte,* 1930:79; *Reyna Almandos,* 1920: 123–132.
43. *Sánchez Viamonte,* 1930: 91; *Terragno,* 1971: 12.
44. *Ayarragaray,* 1930: 104–105.
45. *Muello,* 1916: 121; *Reyna Almandos,* 1920: 11; *La Nación,* 12 October 1922: 4; *Reyna Almandos,* 1920: 79–80; *Sánchez Viamonte,* 1930: 74; *Reyna Almandos,* 1920: 89–90; *Muello,* 1916: 71.
46. *La Nación,* 12 October 1922: 4; *Sánchez Sorondo,* 1923: x–xi; *Reyna Almandos,* 1920: 89–90; *Sánchez Viamonte,* 1930: 74; *Ayarragaray,* 1930: 104–105; *Reyna Almandos,* 1920: 17, 116.
47. *Muello,* 1916: 99.
48. *Corallini,* 1931: 178–179; *Reyna Almandos,* 1920: 17, 74, 116; *Ayarragaray,* 1930: 104–105.
49. *Tribuna Demócrata* 4 December 1946: 4; *Martínez Estrada,* 1956: 50–51.

CHAPTER 7

1. Interview, 1972.
2. *Concatti,* 1972: 81.
3. 1951: 117.
4. 1971: 70.
5. Interview, 1972.
6. *Concatti,* 1972: 82.

7. Interview, 1972.

8. That Argentinian society might have shown itself more tolerant than this view predicted may be the conclusion which could be drawn from the case of Regina Paccini, the opera singer who became the wife of President Alvear in the 1920s. Two considerations, however, qualify any comparison between Paccini and 'la Duarte': Alvear himself not only held a position of orthodox power but he had the further advantage of a family of the highest possible social position in Argentina. Also, Paccini showed herself willing to take on the classic role of President's wife. While the object of discrimination at first, she was in the end accepted by high society when she conformed to its standards.

9. Cf. *Mosca*, 1946: 127.

10. See for example *Gazzera*.

11. *Perón, E.*, 1951: 122, 193–194.

12. See *Cossa, et al.*

CHAPTER 8

1. *Hertz*, 1970b; *van Gennep*, 1908 and 1909.

2. *Hertz*, 1970a.

Bibliography

JOURNALS AND UNPUBLISHED WORKS

Ahora

Así

Las Bases

Copi. *Eva Perón*. Unpublished carbon copy. Anonymous translator

Crónica

Daily Mirror

Democracia

La Epoca

El Hogar

El Laborista

Mundo Infantil

Mundo Peronista

La Nación

Noticias Gráficas

El Obrero Ferroviario

La Opinión

Perón, Eva. Speeches. Unpublished collection. Dirección General de Prensa, Subsecretaria de Informaciones, Presidencia de la Nación. 1946–1952.

La Prensa

Panorama

Primera Plana

El Pueblo

Radiolandia

La Razón

The Times
Tribuna Demócrata
La Vanguardia

GENERAL WORKS

Acossano, Benigno (1955) *Eva Perón: Su verdadera vida.* Buenos Aires: Editorial Lamas.

Arcieniegas, Germán (1956) *Entre la libertad y el miedo.* 8th ed. Buenos Aires: Editorial Sudamericana. First published Mexico, 1952.

Aristondo, Angel (1949) *Por la senda de Perón.* Buenos Aires: n.p.

Ayarragaray, Lucas (1930) *Cuestiones y problemas argentinos contemporaneos.* Buenos Aires: J. Lajouane and Cia.

Baily, Samuel L. (1967) *Labor, Nationalism, and Politics in Argentina.* New Brunswick: Rutgers University Press.

Barnes, John (1978) *Evita—First Lady. A Biography of Eva Perón.* New York: Grove Press.

Barth, Fredrik (1959) *Political Leadership Among Swat Pathans.* London: The Athlone Press.

Basualdo, Ana, 'Eva Perón: 20 años después'. *Panorama,* 20 July 1972: 26–29.

Bateson, Gregory (1958) *Naven.* Stanford: Stanford University Press.

Boizard, Ricardo (1955) *Esa noche de Perón.* Buenos Aires: Editorial De-Du.

Borroni, Otelo and Roberto Vacca (1970) *La vida de Eva Perón.* Vol. I: *Testimonios para su historia.* Buenos Aires: Editorial Galerna. This work was to consist of two volumes, but the second, consisting of materials to supplement the chronology and testimonies of the first has not yet appeared.

Bourne, Richard (1970) *Political Leaders of Latin America.* New York: Knopf.

Branchini, Lia Casas de (1953) *Las hadas buenas.* Buenos Aires: Editorial Luis Lasserre.

Burgin, Richard (1970) *Conversations with Jorge Luis Borges.* Discus Books. New York: Avon Books.

Cámaras de Diputados y Senadores de la Nación, *Diarios de Sesiones.*

Capitski, Jorge. 'La prehistoria de Eva Perón.' *Todo es Historia*, June 1968: 8–21.

Celesia, Ernesto (1954) *Rosas: Aportes para su historia*. Buenos Aires: Peuser.

Ciria, Alberto (1971) *Perón y el justicialismo*. Buenos Aires: Siglo 21.

Compañy, Francisco (1954) *Eva Perón: La abanderada inmovil*. Córdoba: n.p.

Concatti, Rolando (1972) *Nuestra opción por el peronismo*. 2nd ed. Mendoza: Publicaciones del movimiento Sacerdotes para el Tercer Mundo.

Congressional Record: see Cámaras de Diputados y Senadores de la Nación.

Coomaraswamy, A. K. (1942, rpr. 1967) *Spiritual Authority and Temporal Power in the Indian Theory of Government*. New Haven: American Oriental Society (rpr. New York: Kraus Reprint Corporation).

Corallini, Enrique (1931) *Formas y enseñanzas de la ultima crisis en la República Argentina: Dos épocas—dos gobiernos*. Buenos Aires: Rasso.

Cossa, Roberto, Germán Rozenmacher, Carlos Somigliana and Ricardo Talesnik (1970) *El avión negro*. Buenos Aires: Talia.

Costanzo, Francisco (1948) *Evita: Alma inspiradora de la justicia social en América*. Buenos Aires: Castroman, Orbix y Cia.

Cott, Nancy F. (1977) *The Bonds of Womanhood: 'Woman's Sphere' in New England, 1780–1835*. New Haven: Yale University Press.

Crisostomo, Isabelo T. (1973) *Marcos the Revolutionary*. Quezon City: J. Kriz.

Damonte Taborda, Raúl (1955) *Ayer fué San Perón: 12 años de humillación argentina*. 2nd ed. Brazil: 1954; rpr. Buenos Aires: Ediciones Gure.

Díaz Iverson, Jorge 'Eva Perón'. *Favoritos de la Historia*, 3 July 1969: 11–14.

Douglas, Ann (1977) *The Feminization of American Culture*. New York: Alfred A. Knopf.

Echeverría, Esteban (1958) *La cautiva: Seguido de El matadero—La Guitarra—Rimas*. 6th ed. Buenos Aires: Editorial Sopena Argentina. 'El matadero' was first published in 1840.

Eloy Martínez Tomás (1970a) 'Eva Perón, semidiosa de Hollywood'. *Panorama*. 24 February 1970: 43–44.

—— (1970b) 'Teatro: Los muertos que vos mátais'. *Panorama*, 23 March 1970: 44–46.

Faron, L. C. (1964) *Hawks of the Sun: Mapuche Morality and its Ritual Attributes*. Pittsburgh: University of Pittsburgh Press.

Fayt, Carlos S. (1967) *La naturaleza del peronismo*. Buenos Aires: Viracocha.

Flores, María (pseudonym for Mary Main q.v.) (1952) *The Woman with the Whip: Eva Perón*. New York: Doubleday and Company.

Franco, Luis (1945) *El otro Rosas*. Buenos Aires: Editorial Claridad.

—— (1958) *Biografía patria: Visión retrospectiva y crítica del reciente pasado argentino*. Buenos Aires: Editorial Stilcograf.

Gálvez, Manuel (1940) *Vida de don Juan Manuel de Rosas*. Buenos Aires: El Ateneo.

García, Eduardo Augusto (1971) *Yo fuí testigo: Antes, durante, y después de la segunda tiranía*. Buenos Aires: Luis Lasserre Editores.

Gazzera, Miguel (1970) 'Nosotros, los dirigentes'. *Peronismo: autocrítica y perspectivas*. By Miguel Gazzera and Norberto Ceresole. Buenos Aires: Editorial Descartes.

Ghioldi, Américo (1952) *El mito de Eva Duarte*. Montivideo: n.p.

—— (1956) *De la tiranía a la democracia social*. Buenos Aires: Ediciones Gure.

Gillone, Elsa G. R. Cozzani de (1953) *Mensaje de Luz*. Buenos Aires: Angel Estrada y Cía.

Goldar, Ernesto (1971) *El peronismo en la literatura Argentina*. Buenos Aires: Editorial Freeland.

Halperín, Tulio (1961) 'Crónica del periodo'. *Argentina 1930–1960*. Buenos Aires: Editorial Sur.

—— (1970) *El revisionismo histórico argentino*. Siglo veintiuno editores.

Hanglin, Fernando 'Aquí yace Eva Perón'. *Panorama*, 12 January 1966: 3–16.

Harper, Edward B. (1969) 'Fear and the Status of Women'. *Southwestern Journal of Anthropology*, Volume 25.

Hennessy, Alastair (1969) 'Latin America'. In *Populism: Its Meanings and National Characteristics*. Ghita Ionescu and Ernest Gellner, eds.

Hertz, R. (1970a) 'Sainte Besse: Etude d'un culte alpestre'. *Sociologie réligieuse et folklore*. Paris: Presses universitaires de France
—— (1970b) 'Contribution à une étude sur la représentation collective de la mort'. *Sociologie réligieuse et folklore*. Paris: Presses universitaires de la France.

Ibarguren, Carlos (1961) *Juan Manuel de Rosas: Su yida su drama, su tiempo*. 1930; rpr. Buenos Aires: Ediciones Theoría.
Imaz, José Luis de (1962) *La clase alta de Buenos Aires*. Investigaciones y trabajos del Instituo de Sociología. Buenos Aires: Imprenta de la Universidad de Buenos Aires.
Irazusta, Julio (1952) *Ensayos históricos*. Buenos Aires: La voz del Plata.
Iriarte, Tomás de (1946) *Memorias*. Vol. 5: Luchas de unitarios, federales y mazorqueros en el Río de la Plata. 2nd ed. Buenos Aires: Ediciones Argentinas Sociedad Impresora Americana. Written 1835–1847; not published until 1946.

Landes, Ruth (1971) *The Ojibwa Woman*. New York.
Langer, María (1966) *Fantasías eternas: A la luz del psicoanálisis*. 2nd ed. Buenos Aires: Ediciones Hormé.
Leach, E. R. (1961, rpr. 1963). *Rethinking Anthropology*. London: The Athlone Press.
Libro negro de la Segunda Tiranía (1958) Comisión Nacional de Investigaciones (Julio Noé, Julián Duprat, Joaquín Otero, Juan Tomás). Buenos Aires: Fiscalía Nacional de Recuperación Patrimonial.
Lombille, Román J. (1956) *Eva, la predestinada: Alucinante historia de éxitos y frustraciones*. 2nd ed. Buenos Aires: Ediciones Gure.
López, Vicente Fidel (1957) *Historia de la República Argentina: Su origen, su revolución y su desarrollo politico hasta 1852*. 1883–1892; 5th ed. Buenos Aires: Editorial Sopena Argentina.
Luna, Felix (1971) *El 45: Crónica de un año decisivo*. Buenos Aires: Editorial Sudamericana.
Lux-Wurm, Pierre (1965) *Le Péronisme*. Paris: Librairie general de droit et de jurisprudence.

Main, Mary (1956) *La mujer del látigo: Eva Perón*. Translated by Augusto Jordán. Buenos Aires: Ediciones La Reja.

Mansilla, Lucio V. (1925) *Rozas: Ensayo histórico-psicológico.* 1898; 2nd ed. Buenos Aires: 'La Cultura Argentina'.

Mármol, José (1887) *Amalia: Novela histórica americana.* 1851; rpr. Paris: Libería de Garnier Hermanos.

—— (1917) *Manuela Rosas: Razgos biograficos*, 8th ed. Buenos Aires: Empresa Administradora y Reimpresora de Obras Americanas.

Mármol, José, Florencio Varela and Esteban Echeverría (1913) *La manía del satanismo politico bajo la dictadura de Rosas.* Buenos Aires: Librería 'El Gran Sarmiento'.

Martínez Estrada, Ezequiel (1946) *Radiografía de la pampa.* 3rd ed. 1933. Buenos Aires: Editorial Losada.

—— (1956) *¿Qué es esto?* Buenos Aires: Editorial Lautaro.

Martínez, Paiva Celina R. de, and María Rosa Pizzuto de Rivero (1967) *La verdad: vida y obra de Eva Perón.* 2 vols. Buenos Aires: Editorial Astral.

Moffat, Alfredo (1967) *Estrategias para sobrevivir en Buenos Aires:* Buenos Aires: Editorial Jorge Alvarez.

Mosca, Enrique M. (1946) *Unión, democracia y libertad.* Buenos Aires: Juan Perrotti.

Muello, Ernesto (1916) *¿Regeneradores? . . . No, mistificadores.* La Plata: n.p.

Murray, Luis Alberto n.d. *Viva y obra de Eva Perón: Historia gráfica.* Buenos Aires, n.p., no page.

Naipul, V. S. (1972a) 'The Corpse at the Iron Gate'. *New York Review of Books*, 10 August 1972: 3–8.

—— (1972b) 'Borges'. *New York Review of Books*, 19 October 1972: 3–6.

National Commission of Investigations: see *Libro Negro de la Segunda Tiranía.*

Ocampo, Victoria (1945) *A las mujeres argentinas.* Buenos Aires: Ed. Sur.

Ortner, Sherry B. (1973) 'Is Female to Male as Nature Is to Culture? *Woman, Culture, and Society.* Michelle Zimbalist Rosaldo and Louise Lamphere, eds.

Paul, Lois (1973) 'The Mastery of Work and the Mystery of Sex in a Guatemalan Village'. *Woman, Culture, and Society.* Michelle

Zimbalist Rosaldo and Louise Lamphere, eds. Stanford: Stanford University Press.

Peña, Milcíades (1971) *Masas, caudillos, y elites: La dependencia argentina de Yrigoyen a Perón.* Buenos Aires: Ediciones Fichas.

Perelman, Angel (1961) *Como hicimos el 17 de octubre,* Buenos Aires: Ediciones Coyoacán.

Perón, Eva (1951) *La razón de mi vida.* Buenos Aires: Ediciones Peuser.

—— (1971) *Historia del peronismo.* Buenos Aires: Editorial Freeland.

Perón, Juan (1970a) 'Las memorias de Juan Perón: 1895–1945'. *Panorama,* 14 April 1970: 21–22.

—— (1970b) 'Las memorias de Juan Perón: Habla sobre Eva Perón'. *Panorama,* 21 April 1970: 66–67.

—— (1971) *Conducción politica.* Buenos Aires: Editorial Freeland.

Pescatello, Ann (1973) Introduction *Female and Male in Latin America: Essays* Ann Pescatello., ed. Pittsburgh: University of Pittsburgh Press.

Raggi, Angela (1953) *Pueblo feliz.* Buenos Aires: Editorial Luis Lasserre.

Ramos, Mejía, José María (1927) *Rosas y su tiempo.* Complete Works, Vols. 1–3, 1907, 3rd ed. Buenos Aires: Editorial Científica y Literaria Argentina Atanasio Martínez.

Repetto, Nicolas (1952) Editorial. *Nuevas Bases,* 5 August 1952: 2.

Reyna, Almandos, Luis (1919) *Hacia la anarquía, examen de la política radical.* Buenos Aires: El Ateneo.

—— (1920) *La demagogia radical: La tirania (1916–1919).* 2nd ed. Buenos Aires: El Ateneo.

Rina Rodríguez, Angela (1949) *Eva de América: Madona de los humildes.* Buenos Aires: n.p.

Rivera Indarte, José (1930) *Rosas y sus opositores.* 1843: rpr. Buenos Aires: El Ateneo.

Rosa, José María (1964) *Historia argentina.* Buenos Aires: Oriente.

Rosaldo, Michelle Zimbalist (1973) 'Woman, Culture, and Society: A Theoretical Overview'. *Woman, Culture and Society.* Michelle Zimbalist Rosaldo and Louise Lamphere, eds. Stanford: Stanford University Press.

Sacquard de Belleroche, Maud (1972) *Eva Perón: La Reine des sanschemises.* Paris: La Jeune Parque.

Saldías, Adolfo (1968) *Historia de la Confederación Argentina*. Buenos Aires: Editorial Universitaria de Buenos Aires.

Sánchez Sorondo, M. G. (1923) *Historia de seis años*. Buenos Aires: Agencia General de Librería [1923 date of introduction].

Sánchez Viamonte, Carlos (1930) *El ultimo caudillo*. Diario El País.

Sánchez Zinny, E. F. (1942) *Manuelita de Rosas y Ezcurra: Verdad y leyenda de su vida*. Buenos Aires: Imprenta López.

—— (1958) *El culto de la infamia: Historia documentada de la segunda tiranía argentina*. Buenos Aires: n.p.

Santander, Silvano (1953) *Técnica de una traición.—Juan D. Perón y Eva Duarte agentes del nazismo en la Argentina*. Montivideo: n.p.

Sarmiento, Domingo F. (1970) *Facundo: Civilización y barbarie*. 1845; rpr. Madrid: Alianza Editoria.

Sebreli, Juan José (1966) *Eva Perón: ¿ aventurera o militante?* Buenos Aires: Edicones Siglo Veinte.

Shack, William A. (1966) *The Gurage: A People of the Ensete Culture*. London: Oxford University Press.

Tejada, Ana Lerdo de and Aurora Zubillaga (1953a) *Un año mas*. Buenos Aires: Editorial Luis Lasserre.

—— (1953b) *Ternura*. Buenos Aires: n.p.

Terragno, Rodolfo (1971) 'El unsufructo de un mito'. *La Opinión*, 29 July 1971: 12.

Valenti, José J. C. (1951) *Cuatro mujeres de la historia americana*. Buenos Aires: n.p.

van Gennep, A. (1908) 'L'action individuelle et l'action collective dans la formation du culte de la sainte vierge'. *Religions, Moeurs et Légendes: Essais d'Ethnographie et Linguistique* 1ʳ serie. Paris: Societé du Mercure de France.

—— (1909) 'A propos de Jeanne d'Arc' *Religions, Moeurs et Légendes: Essais d'Ethnographie et Linguistique* 1ʳ serie. Paris: Societé du Mercure de France.

Villafañe, Benjamin (1922) *Yrigoyen, el último dictador*. Buenos Aires: Moro Tello y Ciá.

Viñas, David (1963a) 'Venganza'. *Las malas costumbres*. Buenos Aires: Editorial Jamcana.

—— (1963b) 'La señora muerta'. *Las malas costumbres*. Buenos Aires: Editorial Jamcana.

—— (1965a) '14 hipótesis en torno a Eva Perón'. *Marcha*, 23 July 1965: 19–20.

—— (1965b) '14 nuevas hipótesis en torno a Eva Perón'. *Marcha*, 3 September 1965: 23–24.

Wadley, Susan S. (1975) *Shakti: Power in the Conceptual Structure of Karimpur Religion*. Chicago: Department of Anthropology, University of Chicago.

—— (1977) 'Women and the Hindu Tradition'. *Signs*, Volume 3, No. 1.

Walsh, Rodolfo (1965) 'Esa mujer'. *Los oficios terrestres*. Buenos Aires: Jorge Alverez.

Wilde, José A. (1966) *Buenos Aires desde 70 años atrás (1810–1880)*. Serie Siglo y medio, 2. 4th ed. Buenos Aires: Editorial Universitaria de Buenos Aires.

Witke, Roxane (1977) *Comrade Chiang Sh'ing*. Boston: Little, Brown, and Co.

Index

The publishers have tried to trace owners of all copyright material, but in some cases it has proved impossible to do so. Please notify us of any omissions so that we may make proper acknowledgement in future editions. The author and publishers acknowledge the following sources for photographs and illustrations. DUST JACKET: Díaz Iverson, Jorge (3 July 1969) *Colleción* No. 1, back cover. FRONTISPIECE: Díaz Iverson (3 July 1969) *Favoritos de la historia* No. 2, p. 3. PAGE ONE of plate section: above left, Borroni, Otelo and Roberto Vacca (1970) *Eva Peron*, paperback series *La Historia Popular*, Buenos Aires: Centro Editor de America Latina, p. 15; above right, *Radiolandia* Vol. XIX No. 905 (11 August 1945), p. 39; below, Díaz Iverson, *Colección*, p. 2. PAGE TWO: *Primera Plana* No. 495 (25 July 1969) p. 31. PAGE THREE: above, Borroni and Vacca, p. 62; below, Díaz Iverson, *Favoritos de la historia*, inside front cover. PAGES FOUR AND FIVE: left, Perón, Eva (1951) *La Razón de mi Vida*, Buenos Aires: Ediciones Peuser, p. 48; centre, *La Razón de mi Vida*, frontispiece; right, Díaz Iverson, *Favoritos de la historia*, p. 4. PAGE SIX: above left, *Así* Vol. XVIII No. 842 (25 July 1972) Buenos Aires: Editorial Sarmiento S. A., p. 8; above right, Rina Rodriguez, Angela (1949) *Eva de America: Madona de los humildes*, Buenos Aires: Editorial Mayo, cover; below, Díaz Iverson, *Favoritos de la historia*, p. 26. PAGE SEVEN: left, *Sunday Mirror* (24 June 1973) London p. 23; right, *Tribuna Demócrata*. PAGE EIGHT: above, *Christianismo y Revolución* Vol. VI No. 30 (September 1971), cover; below, Borroni and Vacca, p. 98.